The Last Indian
or
The Destruction
of Two Cultures

Narindar Saroop

The Last
Indian

or

The Destruction of
Two Cultures

New European Publications
In association with Chanadon Publications Ltd
London 2005

Published in the United Kingdom in 2005 by
New European Publications
14-16 Carroun Road
London SW8 1JT, England

British Library Cataloguing in Publication Data

ISBN 1-872410-47-2

Page Design: Luise Hemmer Pihl
Cover design: orbitgraphic.co.uk
Composed in Book Antikva and Charter BT

Printed in England by
ANTONY ROWE Ltd.
Bumper's Farm, Chippenham
Wiltshire SN14 6LH

Contents

List of Illustrations:

Sir Chottu Ram electioneering on an elephant.
Twentieth Century's first Asian Parliamentary Candidate with past leader.
Cavalry Memorial Sunday, Hyde Park; author centre left.
Royal Ascot 1951 – Churchill with Sir Khizar Tiwana.
On being commissioned into 2nd Royal Lancers (Gardner's Horse).
Sir Sikandar Hyat with Churchill and Field Marshall Lord Wavell, Cairo 1941.
Greenwich 1979 Election Meeting supported by Lord Home.
Sir Sikandar Hyat, Punjab Governor with staff.
The Prime Minister being received at their dinner by author and wife.
British and Princely India 1858-1947 showing the boundaries of Baroda, Cooch Behar and Jaipur.
India post 1947-8.

'He created a plebeian aristocracy and blended it with the patrician oligarchy. He made peers of second rate squires and fat graziers. He caught them in the alleys of Lombard Street and clutched them from the country houses of Cornhill.'

Disraeli - of the Younger Pitt.

Acknowledgements

I am indebted to Sir Richard Body for his encouragement and support.

It is usual to thank the deserving person who has struggled with a handwriting almost illegible, and in this context Amy Boyle must surely be in front of the queue, in step with Luise Hemmer Pihl, for so ably managing the typescript.

Can one thank the dead, parents, family, friends and colleagues, and also enemies, who have enriched one's life?

For
STEPHANIE
who has long endured
The Last Indian

Foreword
by Lord Deedes of Aldington

I like to think that in days gone by we had a special relationship with India, warm and singular, notwithstanding some stormy passages on which authors who never served there have been pleased to dwell. This book is a reminder of those relationships. The author, born and brought up there in the days of British rule, has long made a life here - long enough to understand us better than some of us understand ourselves.

He entered our politics, shared our club life and other eccentricities and still remains fond of us. The reader should not be misled by the words, " the destruction of two cultures". India has won her independence, a battle so oddly waged between Winston Churchill against Stanley Baldwin, and is now on the high road to become a successful nation. What has India got that the African continent lacks? This book offers some enlightenment on that. Naturally, our relations are not so close as they once were, but what India now is has been built on the past, so the past is worth recalling.

No one is better qualified than Narindar to give this portrait of it . It is what we journalists call " a good read", and, as the author's friends would expect of him, refreshingly good-humoured.

Preface

When I was at school, my geography lessons stated that there were about 600 million Chinese, and about 400 million Indians. These populations of course have by now doubled or more.

Eyebrows would therefore be raised, and questions justifiably asked about how I could have the presumption to describe myself as the last Indian. Up to my generation, most Indians like myself in the Punjab were brought up and educated into our scriptures, our culture and our language. We were also educated in English and England's culture at its peak, not the trite and trivial trash into which it has been reduced by the transatlantic intrusion, of Coca Cola synthesis aided by television to reduction into an amorphous state and almost the lowest common denominator. The degeneration and the contrast with England within recent memory is marked. Everything to do with England at the time was a hallmark for excellence. We would have laughed if somebody had mentioned a Japanese made motor car, or suggested that we lunch or dine on that American culinary creation called a hamburger – the very idea! I have consciously used the term 'England' which was in common usage then, in preference to Britain or UK; the latter is said to have originated with some of our diplomats trying to sell England abroad.

We were bilingual from birth, slipping easily from one language into the other. We knew our religion and ancient customs which have held India together for centuries, notwithstanding its

1

size and disparity. We loved and respected these, as much as we did the England that was. I have no embarrassment in saying that at the time we accepted a foreign monarch as our Emperor. In fact, for those with a romantic imagination, it provided a strain of historical interest. It was a perfectly natural thing to witness in my childhood the festivities of King George V's Silver Jubilee in 1935, to see later my father and others wearing black armbands in mourning when he died, and later still to wear another black armband myself, in uniform as a young cavalry officer with my regiment, the 2nd Royal Lancers (G.H.) when King George VI died in 1952, although India was then no longer a part of the Raj. The Regiment was then out in the field, but its tailoring section produced over 600 armbands within a few hours. (Where on earth did they get the cloth out in the wilderness?)

We were brought up in two cultures, Indian and English, and were at home in both. Many years later, the late Sir Iain Moncreiffe of that Ilk told me that historically there was nothing uncommon about this. After the Norman Conquest, the court language in England was French for a long time; after the Act of Union in 1707, the Scottish aristocracy deferred to London, and adopted English ways. Equally so, during the Mughal Empire in India, leading families adopted Mughal culture. It is only because British rule is within living memory that an understandable sensitivity and a chip on their shoulders is why many Indians today do not wish to understand or accept this. Families with property and traditions to guard and to pass on to succeeding generations have always deferred to central authority.

The initiative and move for Indian freedom came from the middle classes, who were much more Anglicised than we were. Of course the peasants and the Punjab aristocracy desired freedom as well, but in an orderly and unhurried fashion. In all fairness it has to be said that the wealthy urban middle classes in the Punjab were far less vociferous in their demands for the British to depart than were their counterparts in the United Provinces, where the Nehru family and others provided a focal and rallying point with chatter about freedom immediately, without giving much thought to what could follow. They would find much in common with the chattering classes of Britain today, whose spiritual home appears recently to have moved from Hampstead to Islington. The vast majority of the people of the villages, who were and still are the real India, were in no hurry to get rid of the British; and apart from a few and unfortunate exceptions the majority of the Princely States were well ruled – the affection and respect that their populations show for their erstwhile rulers is still marked and manifest in India today. Successive British Governments since the First World War dithered and procrastinated about granting India Dominion Status, which was justifiably deserved and expected in the 1920s. I think history will describe it as one of the biggest blunders of the twentieth century, and equally so the refusal of the Indian leaders to accept the offer made by the Cripps mission in 1942. Their refusal to co-operate in the War effort in 1939–45 showed lack of sagacity. This cry for self-government came from those who were desperate for power and therefore the desire to erase the British connection. They set about after 1947 wilfully to destroy the fabric of Indian society, by legislating undue social and agricultural reform, and the creation of states on a linguistic basis to replace the old provinces. It was a veneration of change and so-called progress for its own sake as is again currently happening in Britain. Members of the traditional ruling and governing families were virtually excluded from politics and the corridors of power by subtle means. As an example, the newly formed Indian Foreign Service was initially largely recruited from Nehru's coterie of friends. Even those princes and others who offered India their services for free were spurned at the time. It is not difficult to draw an analogy with the thoughtless and unnecessary recent expulsion of hereditary peers from the House of Lords. I do hope that India will accept the British Raj as a fact of history, as much as the Roman occupation of Britain has been accepted here for centuries. India owes more to Britain that it is fashionable to acknowledge. Its elite schools, universities, its civil service, its army, its press and its parliamentary system all originate from British sources and nurture. Every few generations, throughout history, one class has replaced an earlier one.

But until now, the newcomers accepted and tried to emulate the traditions and values of what existed previously. If you destroy all that totally, as was done in India, and is happening in Britain, the successors to wealth and power have no rules which they can see to follow. They have no heroes, only role models who tend to be celebrities. You got then, in India, a rudderless society without much taste, with gross vulgarity, and with no God but mammon. Whenever I have been obliged, for political or business reasons, to accept social invitations from the new rich, I have wondered about their extreme hedonism, their lack of interest in history, their lack of general compassion, their lack of a sense of duty to those less fortunate than themselves, and particularly their lack of style. Those in a position to make decisions show a lack of maturity in their rush to erase the British connection as shown by the fervour to change the names of cities like Bombay, Calcutta and Madras, each one of them a British creation. (When history is obliterated, truth is vanquished.)

This is the society bequeathed in India to descendants of the zealous reforming forbears. There must be an element of poetic justice in this; the gap between rich and poor is larger, corruption is rampant, and the only duty that most of the new ruling classes recognise is to themselves. On numerous visits to Delhi in the 70s and 80s, comments from villagers, from pensioners of my old Regiment and from taxi drivers, were the same, 'Sahib, it is just as well that you left India; someone like you now could no longer even take a step forward here.'

The Generations since 1947 are not at fault or responsible for the current bazaar levels to which the political and social spheres have been obliged to succumb. Change is inevitable, but it has been too drastic. I feel saddened that only over a generation ago, Indian society had a harmony and stability which produced a civilised vibrancy. Good God! I could as well be talking about Blair's Britain.

My life has been more full of misfortunes than the other way round, but I take some solace and comfort from being of a generation of Indians that has almost gone. We loved the country of our birth and all it had to offer then. We loved England as it was, inspiring the rest of the world with its language, literature, institutions, fortitude, and above all else its freedom of speech, its encouragement of individuality, and particularly its eccentricity. It should then be no surprise that P.G. Wodehouse's largest following in the world flourishes in India today. Indian humour is not as subtle as English humour, but knowing instinctively that laughter is a great gift they like to laugh even when there is nothing to laugh at.

I don't know how else to define The Last Indian. If Bertie Wooster had asked Jeeves to define it, I would love to know the answer.

'The Punjab was a dream', John Glendevon told me once, quoting his father Lord Linlithgow talking about his Viceroyalty. 'It was the most stable province, and better administered than any other territory in the Empire, probably including the Home Country'. The cream of the Indian Civil Service, British and Indian, opted to serve there. It was the granary of India, with a climate although punishing in the summer, judged to be amongst the best anywhere in the winter months, nurturing Punjabi hardihood. Its people were and are a mixture of Aryan, Greek and every Central Asian invader who has passed through it on the way to the spoils offered eastwards by Delhi. A very large percentage of the population belonged to the second tier of the Hindu caste system, one which throughout history has provided the farmers, warriors, rulers and administrators. No wonder that about 90% of the Indian Army was recruited from the Punjab.

There were the three main religions, Hindu, Muslim and Sikh all living in near perfect harmony in towns and villages, participating in each other's festivals, and tacitly admitting to themselves, but not publicly, that they all shared a common ancestry. Until the Muslim invasions from about the ninth century onwards, all had been Hindu; then some converted to being Muslim, and a few centuries later some converted to Sikhism. But they shared the same blood, then and now. Surnames were common between all three, a notable example being the name Tiwana. The only Indian Herald during the British Raj was a Tiwana, and it was Sir Umar who proclaimed Queen Victoria, Edward VII and also George V. His grandson, Sir Khizar was the last Premier of undivided Punjab until 1947. There are Hindu and Sikh Tiwanas, one of them being a Judge of the Indian Punjab High Court until recently.

The Punjab, so called because it was the land of five rivers flowing from their Himalayan sources into the Arabian Sea, had enjoyed a remarkable stability since the mid nineteenth century when the British took it over from the Sikhs. From this time until the transfer of power in 1947, it had on its borders, the deserts of Sind in the south west, Tibet in the north east and the Khyber Pass just over a day's journey away to the north west. It has never had any mineral wealth, and to this day precious little heavy industry. Its fertile soil had been increased in size by the irrigation schemes introduced from about the 1860s onwards, harnessing the Himalayan waters flowing through it. It was the most imaginative and successful irrigation scheme in the world, looked upon as a model by the rest, including America. It has never produced much of renown in the arts or other cultural activities, giving rise to the jibe from other jealous parts of India that the only culture that the Punjab has is agriculture. Whatever we did not have was balanced by the main trait of character that we do have, and that is a sense of humour; earthy maybe but an overwhelming ability and desire to laugh. We would not have fitted into Hitler's concept of the Aryan race.

Its society was mainly clannish cum feudal. There was a strong clannish feeling, at times straddling differences of religion, not very different from having two Plunkets, one Catholic and the other Protestant. The feudal strain was not quite that strong, because the Punjabi character is not naturally inclined to admit or accept another's superiority. Hence there was little servility, but a large measure when deserved of deference and respect mingled with affection, all of which contributed to making good soldiers. As one of the eleven provinces of British India, it had been governed from the early 1920s by the Unionist Party of India, under the system of dyarchy whereby Delhi reserved subjects like Defence and Foreign Policy for itself, but progressively ceded authority over others like Education etc. to Provincial Elected Assemblies. As its name implies, the Unionist Party of India believed that religion should not come into politics, that all had common political interests and objectives without religious differences making waters murky. It had been founded by Hindu, Muslim and Sikh stalwarts, working together. Sir Fazli Hussain, Sir Chottu Ram, Sir Sikandar Hyat Khan and Sir Sundar Singh Majithia all had the same vision. The Punjab was predominantly farming, therefore the interests of the tiller of the soil, the prime producer, came first. The urban middle classes consisting of moneylenders and traders thought otherwise. The local press controlled by them dubbed the Unionist Government as 'Rule by the Squirearchy'. In years of failing monsoons on which the poor farmer depended, almost all his possessions including land could be in hock to the moneylender at extortionate rates of interest. Along with several other pieces of legislation, the Unionist Government removed this evil with its Land Alienation Act, which prohibited anyone other than the tiller of soil from owning any farming land. For about half a century, this was Linlithgow's 'dream province'.

The sub-continent has never been able to achieve unity as one country. In the two most recent Central Powers in Delhi, the Mughals did not control the southern half, the British controlled territory was less than what was described as Princely India. It is sad that let alone being well acknowledged, very few know that the only man who came closest to uniting India was the Marquess of Linlithgow. During his Viceroyalty he was attempting to implement the Government of India Act 1935, passed at Westminster earlier. This envisaged a Federated India, with the existing eleven British provinces and the Princely territories in a Federation where the only powers reserved to the centre in Delhi would be Defence,

Foreign Affairs and Transport. The rest would be entirely delegated, with each constituent completely autonomous for the remaining responsibilities of democratically elected assemblies. Alas! It was not to be. As my father, and years later, John Glendevon told me, the Viceroy was thwarted by two intractable individuals – Gandhi in India, paying lip service, and yet arriving at crucial meetings with the Viceroy, with Agendas earlier agreed, for his acolytes to say 'Your Excellency, the Mahatma has declared today as a non-speaking day'; and in England, Churchill at his most vehement against Indian independence, exhorting the Indian Princes not to federate, egging them on to feel that they would lose all. They were fools to listen to him. Only twelve years later they did lose all to Nehru and his socialism. If they had decided to accept Federation is one of the biggest ifs in Britain's and India's history. When Gandhi was assassinated on 30 January 1948, John Glendevon asked his father whether he was truly a great man. The former Viceroy replied, 'Yes, he was, but he treated me badly'. This was a cri de coeur. When John Glendevon, as Lord John Hope, entered the Commons in the 1945 election, Churchill asked him to be his PPS. Hope refused, and said privately to me years later that it was inconceivable that he would serve a man, great as he was, who with Gandhi had made his father's life very difficult, possibly even hastened his premature death.

Linlithgow's strenuous efforts to bring about Federation had to be abandoned with the declaration of war in 1939. At that time, out of the eleven Indian provinces, nine were controlled by a democratically elected Indian Congress Government. The two exceptions were the Punjab and Sind, the latter by a coalition, and the Punjab by the traditional Unionist party. On 3 September 1939, a number of things happened simultaneously. The Viceroy went on All India Radio to announce that India was at war with Germany; the nine Congress Ministries in the respective provinces resigned saying they had not been consulted; Sir Chottu Ram (my great uncle) in the Punjab went on the air on All India Radio, to announce, 'If Britain fights, the Punjab fight alongside'. In their pique and shortsightedness in resigning power in nine provinces, the Congress Party missed great opportunities, which were to have lasting and serious repercussions some years later. By their policy of non-co-operation in the War Effort, they allowed the Muslim League under Mr Jinnah to become more prominent, shot themselves in the foot by going into the wilderness and denying themselves six years experience of governing and ruling, while the British were still there. I am certain that this would have set a higher tone to their administration after Independence, and India was the loser. Meanwhile, the Punjab went full steam ahead with its War Effort, recruiting being stepped up, War Bonds being sold etc. The two stalwarts of the Unionist Party and in the Punjab Cabinet were Sir Sikandar Hyat Khan (a direct descendant of the man who tried to save John Nicholson outside Kashmir Gate in Delhi in 1857), and Sir Chottu Ram. This strong Hindu–Muslim axis kept Jinnah out of the Punjab. The Punjab was crucial to his concept of Pakistan, the core without which the rest could not exist. He left Lahore chastened in 1944 after a well-publicised meeting with my great uncle, who asked him to define his concept, since in the Punjab there was 'Pakistan' already. The Cabinet had a Muslim majority, as did the Legislative Assembly. He also took issue with Gandhi about the latter's attitude towards the War Effort. I quote from his letter dated 15 August 1944:

'Your policy of non-cooperation should be given up, once and for all. An ounce of Churchill will do the Congress greater good than tons of Chamberlain ... Russia has a greater interest in the spread of its ideology than in the freedom of India ... America has a deeper and more abiding interest in its trade than in India's freedom.'

Sir Chottu was a far-sighted man, given to Churchillian romantic sweeps of imagination. Sadly, the two never met, but Sir Sikandar went to Egypt in 1941 to visit Indian troops, and had a meeting with Winston and Smuts in Cairo. He conveyed a message from my great uncle, with words to the effect that when the time came for the British to leave India, the Punjab should not be partitioned; give it an access to the sea (probably Karachi), and notwithstanding lack of industry it could survive on its own; Punjabi bellies have always been full. Secondly, 'Allow me to re-settle demobilised Punjabi soldiers after the War in the Tigris Euphrates basin. They will turn the land green, and in a crucial geographical position, Britain will have a population basically sympathetic to it'. I remember listening to him at dinner, allowed to sit at table during school holidays, when he said he felt the British would and should leave India around 1965, by which time India would have had time to put its house in order. If this sce-nario had actually occurred, Africa would probably not have 'gone' until the mid-1970s, with corresponding effect on the politics and history of the last four decades of the twentieth century.

Alas! it was not to be. Sir Sikandar died in 1942, and Sir Chottu in January 1945. The Unionist Party, under Sir Khizar Tiwana gamely carried on, but being progressively undermined by Jinnah who was bullying its Muslim members to join his League, and the Congress Party wooing away its Hindu members. In the 1946 elec-tion, the Unionist Party returned without majority to rule, formed a coalition with the Congress, which was short-lived. The then Pre-mier (as they were called) Sir Khizar pleaded the Unionist Case to British delegates at the Paris Peace Conference in 1946, and in San Francisco, but as he said to me in the Cavalry Club a few weeks before he died in 1974, 'My dearest boy, we didn't have to wait for '46 or '47. The moment Labour won the 1945 Election, we knew we had lost, and that Partition was inevitable'.

It was a privilege to have grown up and matured in that ep-och. There was order and no corruption at political levels and prob-ably very little at junior bureaucratic levels. A telling example of the changes was in 1962, on my first visit since 1947, to our erst-while lands in Pakistan. The local Deputy Commissioner enter-tained me to dinner. He had worked under my grandfather (as I referred to Sir Chottu) and my father. He said that in their days when they came on tour, at the end of the day they would turn to all the officers who had been on duty during the day, and say 'I hope all of you will dine with me tonight', whereas in 1962, a Minister in a corresponding situation would look at the faces around him and enquire 'Where am I having dinner tonight?' I told him that the situation was the same over the border in India.

Gandhi said he would rather have chaos than foreign rule, and Jinnah said he must have Pakistan even if it meant bloodshed. Both got their wish.

I hope that in the context of what I have briefly tried to describe I may be allowed to call myself the Last Indian. But then Fate, as often happens, intervened. In 1974, when I was adopted to fight Greenwich for the 1979 General Election, the media's description was the first Asian (I would have preferred Indian) Tory parliamentary Candidate of the twentieth century.

I had suddenly metamorphosed and been catapulted into becoming The First Indian.

Narindar Saroop, CBE

1
Early Life

I was later told that the local band played for a week outside the gates of my father's house in Hoshiarpur. Even at an early age, I am reported to have commented that I hope they played well, seeing that they were being paid to celebrate the birth of the eldest surviving son and heir. An earlier son had been stillborn, when my mother was eighteen, and father twenty-five years old. Although I was subsequently followed by three sisters, one brother, one sister and one brother, in that order, my parents rarely spoke about their first born. It was only through an old family servant that years later I learnt why my mother hated rivers. She would shut her eyes tight every time we drove across a bridge of the Ravi, Beas or Sutlej rivers, three of the five rivers that give the Punjab its name – Punj meaning five, and Ab meaning water – the land of the five rivers. She particularly disliked crossing the Sutlej. My father had then been posted at Ferozepur, a city on its banks and figuring prominently in the Anglo-Sikh wars in the 1840s, and it was here that my elder stillborn brother's infant body had been placed on a small wooden raft and consigned to its current, and if it survived intact past crocodiles etc, to eventually end up in the Arabian Sea, over five hundred miles away, the Sutlej river having joined the mighty Indus en route. According to our ancient customs, all Hindus are cremated after death, but as I subsequently found out, babies are consigned to a river.

Consigning into the holy Ganges is of course preferable, but the Ganges was some hundreds of miles away.

It may not be universally palatable to talk about death, particularly in the first chapter. However, apart from her grief over her first born all her life, she had great inner strength and practicality. In the last few years before she died in 1982, we used to have frank conversations in the family's new house in Chandigarh (the new capital of the Indian Punjab built after 1947 by the French architect, Corbusier, and like his other works, a disaster) about death and the after-life. Our conversation would be in Hindi or Urdu (spoken almost the same, written they are totally different. Like all Aryan script, Hindi is written from left to right, whereas Urdu follows the Arabic pattern, right to left.) She was not educated in English, understood quite a lot of it spoken, but never spoke it herself. Towards the end of her days, sitting out in the garden which she had so capably created and monitored, she would tell me that from the day of my birth she had always wondered and worried about how I would die – her eldest surviving son, with the first stillborn in mind. She knew from my infancy that whatever I did afterwards, I would initially join the family Regiment, 2nd Royal Lancers (Gardner's Horse). This could mean being in war, and possibly killed.

I used to pull her leg. She had a sense of humour, but not as great as my father's. I said, 'Mummy, there are only three honourable ways for a gentleman to die; I am a descendant of the Aryan hordes who came in, conquering, pillaging and raping into the Punjab centuries before Christ; the first one and the most honourable is to die in battle; the second one is to be assassinated because that means you are important; and the third, darling Mummy is to be murdered by a jealous husband.' 'You are a badmash,' she would reply, 'just as bad as your father.' The Urdu word 'Badmash' could be translated as a mixture of rogue, scoundrel and lecher. My father did not fully deserve this affectionate description, although I might have done. He was truly a gentle man, and also one with these two words combined. Nobody could have had a more affectionate, considerate or generous father. He retained his schoolboy sense of humour to the end. Around six feet tall, he had an imposing presence, and unlike me, I saw him lose his temper only about three or four times in his life. He was a good rider, loved games – the modern usage of sport to describe games like football as sport is wrong – as somebody said 'hunting, shooting, fishing and racing are sport, the rest are games.'

We were not particularly rich, just comfortably off. Apart from a few hundred acres of land near our village, Ismaila not far from Delhi, we had a few multiples more in the newly irrigated and fertile lands of West Punjab – now Pakistan – which had made the province the granary of India. Around the 1860s onwards, the new British administration had created a network of canals in this area, from the tapped rivers of the Punjab, the Jhelum, Chenab and of course from the Indus. Until then, it had been more or less arid land, with little recorded ownership, and the government of the day had parcelled it out to those they thought deserving of it, like my forbears, although our original and family lands were over three hundred miles to the east, towards Delhi. Sadly, in India there are few genealogical records kept as faithfully as in England. I have never been able to establish the reason; I can only guess that it is partly the climate against archives surviving, and partly because everyone felt their families had been there for so long that it didn't matter. However, this is no excuse. The late Sir Iain Moncreiffe of that Ilk once told me,' Narindar everyone has a family; some keep records, others do not; those that do are falsely accused of snobbery.' In my own case, there are only two antecedents that I was told about – both by village elders, and it had been carried forward from generation to generation . Given four generations to a century, and accepting that my forbears in India came into the Punjab, to settle near Delhi, and that this migration from Central Asia, Hungary or the Baltic States – all presumed to be, amongst others, the origins of the Aryan race – came in anywhere between 2500 BC to about 700 AD, I was listening to the fact, myth or legend about my first Indian ancestor, either two hundred generations before me, or at the latest, fifty-six generations before I was born.

The story is that my clan, the Jat, described as a martial race, who became settlers and agriculturists settled near Delhi where they were, and still are, a clan divided into sub-clans, after travelling through Afghanistan and the North West Frontier passes towards the fertile Indo–Gangetic plain. The sub-clans are differentiated from each other by a word called 'Goath'. This is rather difficult to explain or describe exactly, but in essence it means consanguinity, inasmuch as all its members are descended from the same person, either man or woman, and therefore forbidden to cohabit.

According to the story, by the time my sub-clan forbears came to within thirty-two miles of Delhi, the patriarch had died, and leadership lay between his two sons – sadly even to this day, the Jats do not practice the rule of primogeniture, which would prevent a lot of family squabbles. When the convoy, or whatever it might be called, camped within thirty-two miles west of Delhi, whoever was responsible made the cardinal blunder of positioning the two 'raths' or chariots containing the respective wives of the two brother leaders next to each other. When the elder brother returned to his chariot in the evening, he was greeted by an angry hysterical wife, who said she would not spend another night within a hundred miles of her sister-in-law, parked next door. Apparently, the wife of the younger brother had been overheard making scathing remarks about the other, and on top of the long-standing tension between them, this was the last straw. The elder brother must have been a weak man, gave into his wife, and the tribe divided that very night. Those who followed the elder brother trekked over a hundred miles south east in the Gangetic plain towards what is now Lucknow, and founded around twenty-three villages surviving to this day. The remnant adhering the younger brother stayed where they were, founding seven villages. To this day, or rather until the mid-1960s when I last discussed the matter with my kith and kin in my village, nobody from one group of villages would be allowed to marry anybody from the other group – partly for reasons of enmity, and partly for reasons of consanguinity. I am descended from the younger brother, the cadet branch as Sir Iain Moncreiffe of that Ilk would call it.

What is not quite such a legend or a myth but nearer fact is a more recent forbear, circa mid-eighteenth century, who lived towards the end of the authority of the Central Power in Delhi, the Moghul Empire. Our village is only thirty-two miles from Delhi, but it is not on the historically famous Grand Trunk Road, which runs for about fifteen hundred miles from Calcutta from the foetid Bengal plains to Peshawar on the North-Western Frontier Province, where the air is anything but foetid – blistering hot in the summer, and bracingly cold in the cold weather. We always used to call it the cold weather season, rather than winter. But, as the crow flies, the nearest point on the Grand Trunk Road would be, and still is, approximately twenty to thirty miles from our village. My seven times grandfather – given twenty-five years per generation, hit upon a simple expedient, following almost exactly the tactics of the Red Indians in the Wild West. Twice a year the Imperial entourage moved along the Grand Trunk Road, in early summer migrating to the cool hills of Kashmir, and in early autumn the reverse journey to Delhi, the Imperial capital. The whole convoy or column was miles long, almost every chariot or waggon containing some valuables. My ancestor rightly calculated that if he and his followers cut off the last waggon in the column, one in the summer and the other in the autumn, he would have enough to live on, and be able to feed the other villages particularly in years of bad or insufficient crops. He got away with it. He was never caught, although living within a day's ride for the Imperial troops from Delhi. It was rivetting to listen to the villagers speculating about how many feasts he had organised.

One day in the 1970s, sitting with my parents in the garden of their house in Chandigarh, with its delicious smells of jasmine and other sweet-smelling plants and trees, my mother was in a testy mood. She had got cross with my father at dinner over something I can't remember. 'Did you know,' she turned to me, 'you who adore your father and his side of the family? You are both descended from "dakoos", bandits and highwaymen.' 'Darling Mummy,' I replied, 'I am rather proud of it, it would get me a few more votes in Greenwich when the next Election is held.' I was then fighting Greenwich for the 1979 Election, and was visiting my parents from England. We all laughed, as we did together very often. 'Be that as it may,' she continued, 'but your father is a fool. He has been spending money, supporting a mad scheme started by your cousin in the village, to dig all round to find the buried treasure your ancestor is supposed to have left behind.' Now this was another myth or legend. Some years earlier, Hari Singh the only son of my father's younger brother, and who lived in the village had come to my father and said he had a dream, in which he dreamt of a serpent under ground guarding the family's missing treasure, accumulated in highly honourable highwayman activities. He thought he knew the actual spot, in the corner of a field near the road and on one side of the family house. My father agreed to back the digging operation financially. Digging started, I think in 1974; my mother died in 1981, my cousin in 1987, my father in 1988, and it continued for fourteen years. I do not know how much it cost, but I saw no benefits.

It was not difficult then to visualise what the village and surrounding land had been like generations earlier, when my ancestor would feed local populations after one of his successful highwayman raids. It had changed little. There was no electricity or running water. A single track tarmac road – in my time – from Delhi skirted it, and with a gentle bend to the right, straightened out again over the railway level crossing, and on its way further north-west towards what is now Pakistan. In the cold weather, from early November to mid-March it enjoyed one of the most healthy climates anywhere – bright and crisp during the day, and frost at night. The early mornings were delightful with the morning haze mixed with the smoke fires hanging low over the fields beginning to ripen with wheat and crops like rape which produces lovely yellow flowers at its top. In the summer, it was harsh, almost brutal. Temperatures hovering around 105°F for weeks, and dust storms. It has been said that the bracing winters gave the local people the hardihood to survive the summers. When there was work to be done in the fields, the men would rise early, and leave after a morning meal of hot milk or tea, accompanied by a thick 'roti', or leavened bread. Towards mid-morning the women would set out for the fields carrying their men's midday meal, which would almost inevitably be some more 'roti', pickle and onions. The late Lord Dunsany who knew Northern India well described it as one of the healthiest diets in the world. Towards evening, the men would be returning from the fields, with again a haze hanging low but with an air of melancholy. They would get back to their houses for an evening meal of several 'roti', again accompanied by hot lentils and more than one glass of milk. Dull it may have been, but healthy their diet certainly was. I can't remember the number of houses in the village, or the population count, both fairly small. All houses were built of caked mud, there was no sanitation, and the gutters in the alleys provided the local sewage system. It may sound offensive in modern terms, and the smells at various times may not have been entirely congenial, but the sun and the heat of the day made their contribution to ameliorating it all. There were only two houses in the village which were not made of caked mud – both belonging to us. The first and older one was in the centre of the village; it was two-storied, if you didn't count the third layer at the top which provided an open roof, spacious and marvellous for sitting around when the sun was not too strong, and for sleeping at night when the weather permitted. Its height and elevated view also had the functional purpose by providing a 360° view for defence purposes when necessary. It really had been necessary before the British brought a settled period from roughly mid-nineteenth century onwards. It had been built more than a hundred years earlier, that is to say around late eighteenth century as a result of my ancestor's looting forays which paid for the bricks and the 'pucca' construction. From the sometimes smelly alley in the centre of the village, you entered a small hall, with a courtyard in front which was open to the elements. There were a few rooms dotted around the court-yard, sparsely furnished with no more than a chair each, sometimes a table, but all had a 'charpoy'; a cot with string to provide the sleeping position. The kitchen was on the ground floor, and as far as I can remember the lady of the house cooked the meals. There were no servants here. On the very few occasions I spent here as a child, we always spent the day on the roof. It was beautiful and bright, the view stretched miles across the flat fields in a clear 360° direction. The railway line to and from Delhi was visible half a mile away, and now and then the thrill of a train – goods or passenger, how many wagons or carriages, how long does it stop at our own railway station eponymously named Ismaila with the village It is a paradox that a village peopled entirely by Hindus for as long as anyone can remember had a Muslim name. The most likely explanation was that it had had a Muslim population when my tribe chose to settle. The original inhabitants were dealt with either according to our martial customs, or 'persuaded to move'. But there is another puzzle as a corollary – how could a village only 32 miles from the Muslim Imperial Capital of Delhi manage to have remained Hindu when forcible conversions to Islam were rampant, particularly in the reign of the last effective Moghul Emperor, Amangzeb who was a cruel fanatic.

As far as I can remember, our immediate family in the village was small – my father's younger brother, my uncle, and his children. My father had two sisters, who had been married off at a young age into families from other villages. As far as I can remember, I never met them or their progeny. I have always been saddened that there are close blood relatives whom I don't know. But there was a rather curious and strange incident in 1991. My poor elder daughter, Vaneeta, experienced the saddest year that any woman could endure – engaged in September 1989 to somebody suitable, wedding bun fights in London and in Delhi, proudly announces in January 1990 that she is pregnant. On 1st November that year her husband dies of a heart attack, in early December she loses her baby. I am proud of her inner strength to have survived all this intact, and at time of writing to be running Conservatives Abroad at Conservative Party Headquarters in London. But, in the intervening time she must have gone through a woman's hell that only a woman can know. Over the next year or more, while she was coping with her grief, a friend and neighbour in Notting Hill took her to a clairvoyant. She told Vaneeta that two ladies who had died sometime ago were looking after her 'from the other side'. Vaneeta enquired about some indications to identity, because there are numerous female relations on her mother's side, but all that could be elicited was that they were from her father's side. My daughter reported the incident to me, and enquired who they could be; for the life of me I couldn't identify who, because there were more dead men in my family than dead women. Then, I suddenly remembered my father's sisters who I had never met. Could it have been they?

Affection and loyalty were very strong in families of those generations. But life in villages like ours in the Punjab, although earthy and jolly, could be brutal, harsh and uncomfortable. There was no inside lavatory in any house; there might have been a small room set aside for bathing, commodious enough for a bucket of water and mug to splash the water over yourself. Other natural functions were performed outside. Before dawn, the whole village could be seen heading for the fields – men in one direction, and women in the other. They used the fields, some carried a 'lota' or vessel of water to clean themselves afterwards, others just used the mud or sand where they were squatting, and washed their hands afterwards. When they later got together, the inevitable repetitious first comment of the day was 'Have you been to the fields?' As a child, I was asked this every day while I stayed there. At first I didn't know what it meant. My father, kindly instructive as always, took me out with him once. 'You will not be obliged to do this often, but you should learn the customs of your village, kith and kin and race,' he said while we were squatting next to each other in one of the fields on our land. Not very different from enquiries amongst our Aryan cousins in Europe, whether either Nanny at home, or Matron at school enquire every day 'Have you been yet?' I must say I never exactly took to it. Births and deaths could also be in the raw. There was no hospital within miles, the nearest dispensary with the most rudimentary facilities and medicines was over two miles away. There must have been a midwife or two in the village, but without any professional training, however with experience picked up on the run. When a pregnant woman's time drew near, quite often she would just walk out into the fields, adopt a squatting position, and deliver. Some experts say this is the best possible position for a woman for an easy delivery. Death could be brutal and unsentimental, at least until the funeral and the mourning afterwards. If people did not die a natural death, in or out of bed, and the individual concerned was either completely infirm or non compos mentis, he or she would be taken out in the fields – what various purposes they served – laid out, and a heavy stone or rock would bash the poor person's head. This unenviable task was performed customarily by the eldest son, or eldest surviving family male member. The cremation would take place shortly afterwards. At the cremation of even those who died in their beds, this custom is still repeated before the funeral pyre is lit. Because I could not get there in time when my mother died in 1981, and my father in 1988, my poor younger brother, then a senior judge, had to perform this grisly and unenviable task, for which he has quite rightly never forgiven me. I think the custom is part of the Hindu belief that the departing soul should escape from the head, and not through any other orifice of the body.

Unlike farms and villages in Europe, there are no outlying or isolated houses connected with Indian villages. The whole population lives close together, goes out to work the land owned respectively by different families, and then returns at dusk. The reason obviously is security, because the whole of the Punjab has been marched over the centuries by various invaders, and there have been several periods when law and order did not prevail. In fact, the only settled period the Province has probably ever known is the British period after circa 1850. But there was one house which stood away from the village, with the main road dividing it from the rest. It stood on the bend, in a commanding position, giving it a clear view of all land around, the railway line and station, and whatever little traffic there was approaching in both directions. This was the family 'Haveli', a word not easy to translate into English. It could mean big house, or biggest house, or a solid or brick-built house, as compared with the other village houses. It was rectangular, if not square with high walls along the tops of which were embedded early versions of razor or barbed wire – sharp jagged pieces of coloured glass potentially harmful enough to deter any intruders. It was no gem of architecture, and not really very old, no more than about 150 years old when I saw it as a child. It had been constructed in the time of my highwayman ancestor, but repaired and strengthened, particularly in my father's time. There was only one entrance, facing the road and large enough to let an elephant through. (Years later, while on an exercise nearby with my Regiment, I had my driver of the Daimler Armoured Car drive through it.) The door was massive, I can't remember what sort of wood, but about nine inches thick, in two sections opening inwards. There were some sort of heraldic carvings on the outside, indicating atavistic nostalgia and our limited artistic sense. But the door was remarkable for the thick metal studs on the outside. They must have been about six inches in diameter converging into a very sharp pointed head, with the object of discouraging enemies with elephants using the latter to batter down the door. Even in my childhood, these were kept sharpened by somebody or the other. If you were able to enter, either on elephant, horse, on foot or in an Armoured Car, you entered a large dusty courtyard with few features to please the aesthete. There were flower beds around, with the inevitable marigolds of Northern India, some roses planted by my mother, along with jasmine. There was no regular or professional gardener as such – one of the locals must have performed this duty unprofessionally. In the centre of the courtyard was furniture best described as the sort that Army officers used to take out when campaigning – a large round table, some reclining chairs, some ordinary chairs, and a large magnificent Hookah. Except during the rainy season, this furniture remained where it was. When we were visiting, it was open house after the evening meal. Those who came early enough managed to find a chair to sit on, others sat on their haunches on the dusty ground around my father. The Hookah would be lit, and conversation flow. I was allowed to sit up as long as I wished or fell asleep, because this was my father's way of letting me absorb and learn the customs of our tribe, which as Aryans has its origins shrouded in the mists of time. The hookah went around in a circle, always clockwise and identical to the ritual of passing the decanters of port and madeira, making me wonder now about some ancient mystical connection.

Questions would fly: "What was my father doing about getting the village more water from the nearest irrigation canal? When was he going to ensure that there was more than one bus per day? What had he done to initiate action against the 'patwari' or village headman in the next village? Yes, it was a good idea to dig a separate well for the scheduled castes (untouchables) in the village; why didn't he leave me behind in the village to be looked after by them (notwithstanding their affection and loyalty, perish the thought). " I would sometimes be sitting in a chair, or sometimes in my father's lap, and there was no political correctness about to stop me having a puff of the hookah – and almost choking on it – while the stem was in my father's hand. These days the local and Brussels health gestapo would prosecute all present for not disinfecting the stem between each smoker. However, the traditional manner of smoking with the stem firmly cupped in one's hand and the smoke only coming through one's fingers was as good an antiseptic or antibiotic or anything else that these bureaucratic bores can find. Not too late at night, our kith and kin would depart. Quite often, our beds were arranged under the open sky. Only those who have slept similarly would fully understand the feelings and questioning in one's mind, all the more mysterious and exciting in a child's mind, as one looked up at the myriads of stars and questioned how, why, when and so on. There were no man-made lights, no noise of traffic, but only man and animals made sounds. The smell of the few fragrant plants planted by my mother would add magic to the sight of the stars above. My mother and father would each have a servant, female and male respectively, who would sit on a low stool towards the foot of the bed, pressing their feet and legs below the knee until they fell asleep, after which the two servants would get up, bow with folded hands in the Indian form of 'namaste', and themselves retire. On the rare occasions that my parents were not asleep within minutes, they would order the servants to retire after five or ten minutes. This was continued until the very end, wherever they were, in 1981 when my mother died with my father following in 1988. In later life, whenever I was home with them, I would perform these duties myself, out of affection and devotion. After my mother died, my father stayed with us on a number of occasions in our London flat in Kensington – no servants here to put my father to sleep. I deputised every night.

While they were falling off to sleep, I would be questioning Bhopal Singh endlessly. He was our chauffeur, a fellow Jat from a neighbouring village. When he wasn't driving us around, I suppose you could call him my male 'nanny'. He looked after my clothes, helped me to dress, etc., played badminton and cricket with me. He was my second and last nanny', the first being an old man called 'Bhura' meaning white, because his colouring was almost white. He was a trusted old retainer, also a Jat, in my grandfather's household. My mother having lost her first son in childbirth had made my grandfather anxious about me when I was born. Bhura was expected to keep an eye on my health and well-being, but quite how he was supposed to do it, I can't say – for he would not have been allowed into my mother's quarters where only female servants could enter. However, he stayed until I was about four and I have such happy memories of his companionship, affection and kindness. However, Bhopal Singh now had to deal with what was obviously a precocious child. Each night I would com-

mand him to answer my questions about how many stars were
there in the sky, and each night I would tell him he was wrong. If
he said he didn't know, I would ask him why didn't he know. One
night he found the perfect answer, with which my father had
briefed him earlier. On being tackled then, Bhopal Singh said,

'Chote Sahib (small Sahib), have you heard of Birbal?'

'Who is Birbal?'

'He was the wise and learned Prime Minster at Emperor
Akbar's Court. His position obviously attracted envy. A few of his
enemies hatched a plot to embarrass him, and to show the Court
that he did not know everything. They went to the Emperor and
petitioned him to ask Birbal how many stars there were in the sky.
His Majesty got into the spirit of the joke, and summoning Birbal
told him that as his Prime Minister knew everything, could he tell
him at once how many stars there were in the sky. His Prime Minister did not hesitate or flinch, but said there were nine million,
nine hundred and ninety nine thousand, nine hundred and ninety-
nine.'

I was silent for a while.

'Bhopal, did His Majesty believe this figure as correct?'

'Do you, Chote Sahib?'

'No,' I said.

'Then if you don't believe me,' said Bhopal Singh, 'count them
yourself, which is what the Prime Minister advised His Majesty.'

Apart from the stars, and the sense of space all around felt
even as a child, I think it must have been then that I learnt to appreciate the silence that prevailed, broken only now and then by
one of the village dogs, or a nearby jackal howling its rather eerie
call. I feel sad when I reflect that in this modern technological age,
generations are growing up, who have never experienced silence,
even in the glorious English countryside, and the uplift it provides
to the mind and the spirit. 'Listen to the silence,' is a rather pro-
found remark I read somewhere. There was a marvellous end to it
at dawn, with the singing of the people drawing water from the
village water wheel, one song for when the buckets went down

to collect, and another a few seconds later when the water was coming up. As much as the morning singing signalled the end of silence, the evening chorus heralded its approach.

We did not spend much time in the village. In all the number of times I was taken there as a child could be counted on the fingers of one hand, and about the same number when I visited it as an adult. The last visit must have been in the late sixties, before I left India permanently. After my first cousin, Hari Singh, died in 1987, there would be nobody left I knew. Of course, the villagers would remember, but there would not be a familiar face. My father, with my agreement, made over the lands and the Haveli to Hari Singh, a sensible decision since he was living there. I was particularly fond of him, there being just over a year's difference in age. It was not until years later when my mother felt that I should know some of the family's secrets, that I learnt that in reality he was my half-brother. My father had been rather naughty with his sister-in-law. Lest this horrifies a number of people, they should understand our Jat clan's customs, brought in by our ancestors when we marched into India, or developed after we settled there. One is our own particular code of chivalry that women must be protected at all costs. In many parts of India, the plight of widows, even today, is a sorry and tragic one. Either neglected or turned out, quite often they turn to prostitution, or become the equivalent of nuns. Not so with the Jats; a brother of the dead woman will take the widow and her children into his household to provide protection and security. This also satisfies our fierce pride that nobody else will touch our women, whatever our own plans and actions may be about those who belong to others.

2
Lahore and Simla

Someone once asked my father which of his seven children he loved the most. He said: "My answer is the same as that of the Viceroy of India", - then the Marquess of Linlithgow, who had five children, and who had said that he loved them all equally. The younger of his twin sons, later to be called Lord Glendevon, became my political mentor and guru, and I had the pleasure and privilege of his deep and abiding friendship until his death in January 1996.

Hoshiarpur (translated literally as the town of the alert, clever or intelligent) the place of my birth was a small town in the foothills of the Himalayas in the province of the Punjab. It is mentioned in ancient scriptures, although no one would regard it in the same holy category as Hardwar or Benares (now Varanasi). My mother had two years earlier given birth to a boy, but still born, and I have sometimes wondered what it would have been like to have an elder brother. My successful delivery was the reason for the festivities.

My family was comfortably off, not rich but important within the context of the times. My father was a District Officer at the time, one of the band of British and Indian civilians who governed India; but the family's relative importance stemmed from the man I called my grandfather, Sir Chottu Ram. He was really my father's uncle, having himself no sons, but only two daughters, one of whom was blind from birth. I think in all he had four nephews, two of whom were his favourites because he saw their potential - but out of these two my father was the preferred one. They both eventually justified his judgement, my father retiring from a responsible senior position in Government, and the other as Speaker of the Punjab Assembly. The birth of an heir (eventually to inherit nothing, financially and politically) was of great importance, and my grandfather sent one of his own particularly selected servants to be in my father's household and to look after me. One of my earliest memories is of him; he was called Bhura (which means very light complexioned) and I suppose therefore that I had a male nanny. In later years with my English contemporaries when we talk about nannies, it is he who comes to my mind.

When I read all the current nonsense spoken and written about the "hereditary principle" I wonder about the lack of sanity on the part of my fellow human beings in their professed, or otherwise, inability to accept facts. We are all a result of the hereditary principle. We are what our forbears bequeathed to us, physical and mental, the spirit being bequeathed by God. I have always supported the "hereditary principle". From my mother I got my fighting spirit and alertness, from my father a sense of history and learning; from both my intelligence and looks.

My father's family were yeoman farmers, settled 32 miles north west of Delhi, descended from one of the later invasions of India from Central Asia. We were, and are, a martial caste called the Jats. Along with the Rajputs, we form the second tier of the four categories in the Hindu caste system - the one providing the fighters and rulers. My mother's family were also Jats, but settled in old Delhi. Although both my parents were married properly within their caste, my father's side looked down on my mother's side as urban, almost traders and in business, whilst my mother's side looked down on my father and his relatives as "peasants". The catalyst in all this had been Sir Chottu Ram who was friendly with my maternal grandfather who lived in Delhi. During one of his visits to Delhi, he saw the daughter of the house, then only around 14, and was taken by her alertness, intelligence and liveliness, ideal for his favourite nephew, my father Ram Saroop, then around 21. A good stock from which to breed the next generation, and I hope that I have not let my grandfather down in his judgement. Both sides were delighted with the arranged match but there was one hurdle. As is the custom in many traditional Hindu families, my mother had been promised years earlier, while still a child, to a boy whose family were acceptable to my maternal grandfather. The latter had to break the news through appropriate intermediaries that the planned wedding was off. This was not well received at the other end. The traditional Hindu wedding follows the ancient custom of the bridegroom's family arriving at the bride's house with a host of relations and others, their party being called a "baraat". In its simplest form, they come, are feasted, various religious and social ceremonies are performed, and they depart with the bride for the bridegroom's family house. These arrangements, which are not always so simple, can at times be financially ruinous for the bride's poor father. When my next sibling, a sister, was married off in Lahore in 1947, the bridegroom's entourage consisted of not only friends and relations but some of their tenants as well. Two separate houses had to be rented for the duration - I can't remember whether it wasn't even three - to provide accommodation for them. They stayed three days.

To return to my parents' match, my maternal grandfather received a threatening message from the aggrieved father of the boy originally engaged to my mother, saying that he would bring his own son's bridegroom party on the wedding day arranged for my mother and father. My grandfather's reply was an exercise in tact and diplomacy - characteristics not inherited in abundant measure by me - "By all means, do come," he replied. "Your party will be fed and entertained like the others, but I shall give my daughter to the other boy."

My mother had tremendous fire and spirit, but only infrequently would she lose her temper. My father was very placid indeed, infinitely patient and gentle - indeed he was the epitome of a gentleman. He had graduated with three languages, English, Urdu

31

and Sanskrit, the last being the ancient Aryan language, followed by a degree in law. But he liked his fun as well. His sense of humour could at times be mischievous, but mostly so in his younger years, when he was also capable of joining in, organising and leading all sorts of riotous activities in which full blooded young men indulge. Often, on returning to Hoshiarpur from a tour (he toured and inspected different parts of his district for about ten days each month) he would not come straight home but go to a friend's house, staying the night there, or more, if the festivities suited him. A number of times he would send for his favourite dishes from his own household, much to my mother's annoyance. She later told me that it was about this time - they had been married for seven years - that she asked herself the question: "If I do not get to control this man, the rest of my life will be a misery". These days they would probably, if not certainly, divorce. But my parents' generation knew better. By skilful female wiles and her will, my mother gradually got the upper hand. After this, and to the end of her days, there was no doubt in anybody's mind, family or servants, as to who was the Commanding Officer of the household.

My parents devoted themselves to their children, resulting in a happy carefree childhood for all of us. I adored my father, but his official duties occupied a great deal of his time, and I resented not having more time with him. One of my earliest memories is sitting on the verandah of our house, overlooking the garden, while the servants brought in my morning glass of milk, and his tray of tea, with a fresh packet of cigarettes on it as well, and a copy of the daily *Civil and Military Gazette* - northern India's local *Times*, on which Rudyard Kipling had once worked. Also present on the verandah would be his barber ready to shave him, and his Personal Assistant, waiting with pencil poised to take any dictation my father wished, or rather was able to while sipping his tea, smoking a cigarette and being shaved all at the same time. And that was not all. Quite often there would be a small queue of people - a mixture of those from our lands or others with petitions for the Government, who would file on to the verandah, one by one.

Where he wished to give an instant decision, he would dictate it on the spot to his PA. This reminds me of my first lesson in humility, I must have been five or six years old, and the queue was long that morning. I was extremely resentful that I would have even less time with my father that day. I walked up and down the queue, shouting "When it is my turn, I will not have people like you coming every morning". At this one of them, an old man with great bearing and dignity looked at me, placed his hand on my head, and said gently: "My child, in that case you will never be our leader, and have the love and respect that your father does". I later discovered that he was a peasant from our village, a fellow Jat, and therefore technically a kinsman, as in the Scottish clan system.

The Jats are one of the warrior classes of India, along with the Rajputs. Of course, the Sikhs and Punjabi Mussalmans - now in Pakistan - are also warrior castes, but they were all originally Jats or Rajputs, having converted once the Muslim invasions started from the north west. To this day, a number of them bear the same clan surname; you can have a Hindu Tiwana or a Muslim Tiwana. As the famous late genealogist, Sir Iain Moncreiffe of that Ilk may have said - they all go back to a common ancestry. Exactly where in the world the Jats originated is lost in the mists of time. Without getting too involved in historical speculations, the Jats were part of the Aryan invasion of India and eventual settlement in its northern parts. These invasions were not just one massed operation at one single moment in history, but several waves coming on, separated by centuries anywhere from 2000BC to the early ADs, and even later. If the origin of the Aryans is not easy to pinpoint, that of the Jats is even more so. All sorts of theories have been put forward in the rather limited written matter on the subject; these suggest obviously Central Asia, less obviously the Baltic states or Hungary. There has been fanciful speculation that the Jats once upon a time ruled the whole area around the Black Sea and territories that are now in Russia. There are many paradoxes in the Jat character. They are extremely hierarchical, and yet will not admit, or even accept, that they are inferior to anyone else, within and without their clan structure. All Jats are equal, but feel that they are superior to anyone else. Their history, such as it is recorded, reveals only a few kings, yet they are not republicans by instinct or temperament. An aristocratic class, although it has existed in a few Jat kingdoms in history, has been more noticeable by its absence, rather than by its presence. Then there is another paradox. Caste, and therefore class, are firmly ingrained in Hinduism. Conversions to Islam and Sikhism were partly occasioned by the desire to escape to a casteless society, as promised by both religions. Yet the aristocracy in old Northern India, now encompassing Pakistan, is or has been mainly Muslim or Sikh; and the vast majority of these in those territories are converts from the original Hindu Jats. In both these religions the converts, descended from the original Jats or Rajputs, to this day tend to look down on and shun fellow religionists not so descended. One of the last princely states in Northern and Central India to fall to the British was the Jat state of Bharatpur in 1825, and it was more by internal treachery than by superior martial force and strategy on part of the British. Their earlier attempt under Lord Lake to subdue Bharatpur in 1810 had been a failure,

I discovered at a very early age the arrogance and pride of my kith and kin - clansmen all; I could not have been more than five or six years old. My father by then had his first car, a Ford, and one day decided to visit our village and lands, approximately two hundred and thirty miles away. My mother hated going there; I did not know what it was going to be like. Never having been in our village, let alone lived in it, I still remember my shock. As we drove up outside our family Haveli , the whole village gathered as the car came to stop in a cloud of dust. My father left the car to go and spend a bit of time with the village elders, my mother and I refused to budge from the security of the vehicle, with the driver and servant remaining with us. I hasten to add that there was no question of anything threatening. The crowd gathered nearer and nearer the car - they had never seen one before. The nearest to the car was a woman, with a baby on her hip, and another child holding her hand. All of them, including many others present would have benefited by cleaning their noses. The child started to run his finger along the car bonnet, and this proved too much for me. I could easily have told the servants to stop it, but got out myself instead, and shouted at them. They moved not an inch - stony silence until the mother shouted out to her child; "He is the same as we are; his blood and skin are the same; go and touch your relation". I fled back into the car, not exactly displaying Jat martial valour. But I have never forgotten the lesson I learnt that day. It fills me still with fierce pride that Jats will not bend their knee to anybody.

Our courage, pugnaciousness and tenacity has been well documented in British Indian military history annals. If the Gurkhas are to be excluded for this particular count, the prepondering majority of the Victoria Crosses and other decorations for valour have been won by Jats, whether Hindu, Muslin or Sikh. I will describe this in greater detail later, including their qualities of endurance, initiative and willpower in the case of those who escaped from German prisoner of war camps in Italy and Germany in World War II, made their way across occupied France into Spain, with their colour and lack of local language stacked against them.

We lived in Lahore in the Winter, and Simla in the Summer, both being respectively the seasonal capitals of the Government of the Punjab, with Simla additionally as the summer seat of the Government of India. The moves were great fun for us children. One set of clothing was packed away, another brought into use. In fact, the sets of clothing required were often left in the two houses, in the hills and on the plains. A few servants would go on ahead to get the respective houses ready, and we would follow to arrive with virtually no unpacking or settling required. Houses in both places were fully stocked, when not occupied were left with a skeleton staff, and always unlocked. Everything was rediscovered as one had left it, notwithstanding the gap of six months in each occupation. I remember the Simla Chief of Police telling me that in 1947 there had been only one murder in his district since the beginning of the century.

Nobody would have described my father as a "speed merchant" on the roads, in fact he never learned to drive. Until he acquired his first car, he had always carried out his district duties on a horse, and returning one day to Hoshiarpur, his horse shied quite near the house, he was thrown off, but his right foot remained entangled in the stirrup. He was then dragged along the ground until the horse came to a stop near the house. He suffered from shoulder pains for many years afterwards. However, our driver was never allowed to exceed 30 mph. My father always liked to sit in front with the driver, and in my early years I used to sit on his lap. His eye would not be so much on the road ahead, but on the speedometer - God help the driver if it touched 31 mph. He would like the window open. I didn't, because it blew my hair - I have always had a horror of looking untidy - he had his solar topee on even in the car. One particular journey when he probably tired of my constant pleas "Daddy, please draw up the window", he said: "Darling Sonny" (which was his way of address to me until he died in 1988, and I was well into my advanced youth) "Lord Linlithgow was recently on a tour, and he didn't mind his hair being blown". This silenced me forever. If it was good enough for the Viceroy, it had to be good enough for me. Only forty years later did I find out from Lord Glendevon, the Viceroy's younger twin son, that his father also kept his hat on when sitting in a car.

The journey from Lahore to Simla or in reverse was a distance of some 225 miles on the Grand Trunk road, plus 56 miles of one of the most successfully engineered mountain roads. There would be bullock carts and *tongas* on the road, but little motorised traffic. We would recognise almost every other car we passed, and its occupants. It used to take us twice as long as it should have done because of the speed limit imposed by my father. We would probably spend two, or even three, nights en route, either in Government rest houses or with friends. With the latter, one may or may not have been expected, in typically Indian fashion. We - that is two car loads of family and servants - just arrived and were made welcome. With the rest houses, which were basic bungalows along the route to accommodate the Government's officers, the *chowkidar* or caretaker would soon work marvels. A local cook would appear and cook a perfectly edible meal. Beds or *charpoys* (cots with strings) would be ready, and positioned outside if the weather permitted. If sleeping outside, I used to love trying to count the stars - in the days before pollution the sky and the stars were so bright that I felt my hands could reach up and grasp them.

The first sight of the Himalayas on the way up to Simla will forever remain ingrained in my memory - the majesty of the high silhouettes of those ranges stirred something deep within me from the age of five, never to be forgotten, almost a stirring of inner spirit. Then, the slow ascent to Simla at a height of between 6,000 and 8,000 feet above sea level - the beautiful ever changing scenery, the smell of the Himalayas after the hot air of the plains. I remember to this day that the first pine tree is, or now maybe was, six miles after the road started ascending. After that it was Alpine smells.

The searing heat of the Punjab plains had never appealed to me, and much as I love the Punjab it has been a stroke of good fortune that I've never had to spend more than a few years enduring its summer heat. Rudyard Kipling, in so much that he wrote about India, expresses this evocatively in his 'Ballad of Burial'.

The Ballad of Burial
I could never stand the Plains
Think of blazing June and May
Think of those September rains
Yearly till the Judgement Day!
I shall never rest in peace
I shall sweat and lie awake
Rail me then, on my decease

To the Hills, for old sake's sake.

It is remarkable how well Kipling understood India and brought it to life in his works. The following extract catches exactly the dedication to duty of the Postal fast service which brought the post to the Hills:

The Overland Mail
Is the torrent in spate? He must ford it or swim
Has the rain wrecked the seed? He must climb by the cliff
Does the tempest cry halt? What are tempests to him?
The service not a 'but' or an 'if'
While he breathes in his mouth, he must bear without fail
In the name of the Empress, the Overland Mail.

It is difficult to describe how much I have loved Simla all my life. When many years later, I first went to Baden-Baden in Germany, it was so reminiscent of it - orderly, beautiful, well laid out, pervaded with an aura of command, dignity, manners, grace and courtesy. The only difference was that Baden-Baden was mainly festive, while Simla was the seat of the Indian Empire. For six months of the year, no city other than London could have been so important in the British Empire. There was the Viceroy, the Commander-in-Chief, and the Governor of the Punjab with his Cabinet, of which my grandfather was the second, if not the most prominent member. There was no motor traffic allowed in those days, except for the Viceroy, Commander-in-Chief , and the Punjab Governor, but even they very rarely used their cars. Everyone either walked, rode, or had their rickshaws, the personal ones individually designed like carriages were, and carried by two men in front, and three in the rear - the usual ones plying for hire had only two men pulling at the back. Most families dressed their rickshaw personnel in personal livery. I still remember a number of them. The Viceroy's were scarlet and gold, and my grandfather's maroon and rather muted gold. A striking combination of white and green were the colours of the Tiwana family, Sir Khizar Hyat Tiwana's father having been the only hereditary Indian herald. Three generations of Tiwanas at various times proclaimed successive English sovereigns as Empress or Emperor of India.

Simla was a dream. Our house was called Benmore, with its own tennis courts. After the heat and dust of the plains, I recall the joy of waking up in Simla on the first morning there - the smells of the Himalaya deodar trees, the gentle mountain sounds and the peace.

The house in Simla, though large enough, was not as spacious as the one in Lahore - and there was certainly one deficiency. The Simla house only had one kitchen, whereas the one in Lahore had three. In descending order, there was the one for my mother and my grandmother on her side; both strict vegetarians. In those days their cook had to be a female Brahmin - the purest of the pure. Next in line was my father's kitchen, a carnivorous one, with the most marvellous cook, Bachan Singh, who I shall never forget. The third kitchen was for the servants and for people from our village and thereabouts who used to flock into Lahore sometimes to pursue their litigation in the High Court, or merely to say: "I am only here to pay my respects to His Excellency the Governor and to you". These people had nowhere else to stay - could not afford to. So there they were, and I think they were accommodated in six or seven single rooms as outhouses provided with all the facilities, but no bedding. My mother would do anything else for them but she was not going to provide linen for the great unwashed, worthy though they were in so many ways. Before I was sent away to school, I used to have the run of all three kitchens. Twice a day, I would dart into each, sampling and enjoying every tasty, but different, morsel they had to offer. I would then decide from which my meal would come - sometimes all three - and give instructions accordingly to my servant. Let me say that my mother ran the house perfectly. Each of my brothers and sisters had their own personal servants, separate from the household staff, although of course they mucked in and helped in general duties. The run of the three kitchens has given me the blessing of a developed and discerning palate for genuine and properly home cooked Indian food, totally different from what is served in most Indian restaurants, and five star hotels in India and around the world. There is no such word as curry in India; each dish has its own distinct name.

There are so many abiding memories of Simla. Even if I could describe them adequately I would not wish to, because many cherished things diminish in the telling. There has been enough written about it in so many books about the Raj. Suffice to say that today it is a heartbreak. In whatever way the world may have improved in the second half of the 20th century, medicine for instance, it has certainly not advanced in taste. A number of beautiful things have been destroyed in the interest of sheer greed and tastelessness, and not for the first time in history, the barbarians and vandals appear to have taken over. But, one last memory of family life in Simla. My younger brother by eight years, then a very small child, seemed to have a penchant for urinating outside in nature. He was quite right. Most gentlemen prefer to do the same without being observed. It is inexplicable, but it is that much more satisfying outdoors, under the trees, sky and stars. His mistake, poor boy, was at that age not knowing how to do it and get away with it. He didn't; punishment was as gentle as it could be in a loving household. He is, at the time of writing in 1999, a Judge of the High Court in Simla, fittingly living in the same old house, Benmore, once the scene of his urinary depredations.

We were in Simla, when the Second World War broke out in September 1939. I remember so well, standing with my father at a place called Scandal Point on the Mall, with luminaries like the Premier of the Punjab, speculating on how long the Poles could hold out against the Germans. I remember later that year - but by that time we were back in Lahore - the feeling of some celebration that the German battleship *Graf Spee* had been sunk - one particular reason of elation was that one of the Officers on board one of the Royal navy ships that was responsible - I think it was *HMS*

Achilles - was the son of a colleague of my father's, Brigadier Brayne. It must have been the following year, or in 1941 before the annual Summer exodus to Simla that my grandfather decided to go on an inspection tour to the Tibetan border. In those days, the Punjab stretched from Rawalpindi near the North West Frontier in the West, to Delhi in the East, and to Tibet in the North - it was all just one province, one administrative entity. Nowadays, that territory is composed of the Pakistani Punjab, the Indian Punjab, Haryana and the hill tracts known as Himachal Pradesh - four administrative entities. That means four times the political and bureaucratic set up, and many times more the corresponding cost. However my grandfather's responsibilities as a member of the Punjab Cabinet required him to look at the Indo (Punjabi in the North Western section of it) Tibetan border. Most, if not all, of his tour was going to be on horseback, so he left behind his Chevrolet car with my father until his return, taking among his staff his chauffeur, the faithful Muni Ram (after my grandfather's death in 1945, Muni Ram became the head chauffeur on the staff of the Governor of the Punjab, Sir Bertrand Glancy); Muni Ram also doubled up as my grandfather's valet and personal manservant. The Governor's car had no number plate, only a crown: the car belonging to the Premier (as he was officially called) of the Punjab, Sir Khizar Hyat Tiwana was numbered PB (i.e. Punjab) 1, and my grandfather's car number was PB2, with our selves way down the line on PB77. The Chevrolet was therefore left in our garage looked after by my father's driver, Bhopal Singh. Bhopal, a fellow Jat from a neighbouring village, was even more one of the family than the rest of the servants were. We children all loved him for his patience and affection for us, to the extent that one day my third sister, Bimla ran to him and clasped him, crying: "Mummy has scolded me, you are my only friend". To get back to my grandfather's car, one day I told Bhopal Singh to take it out of the garage, and drive me around Lahore. He did this most unwillingly, rightly grumbling he should get permission first etc. When we drove out of the house, I ordered him to unfurl the Ministerial flag on the bonnet of the car, really only to be done when my grandfather was riding in it. We sailed along happily while driving sedately along the Mall, which stretched approximately three miles from the Secretariat, past Kim's Gun (Rudyard Kipling) to the military cantonments. I was enjoying every moment of it - savouring what it would be like to be one of His Majesty's Ministers in the Punjab being saluted by one or two policemen on traffic duty on the way when there was a rude awakening. A huge motor bicycle, I think it was a Harley Davidson, used those days by all the police sergeants on duty, roared past us waving us down to stop. We did. He got off, and motioned Bhopal Singh to step outside. The Punjab Police non-commissioned ranks those days had a very large number, if not all its full complement, of former British Army NCOs and Anglo Indians. By and large, they did their job well. This particular one who had ruined my drive and reverie admonished Bhopal Singh, who poor chap was trying to explain, pointed to me inside. The sergeant walked up to my window; I stood my ground, or rather continued sitting in a grand pose, although quaking inside.

The conversation went something like this:

    Sergeant: "Is this your car?"

    Answer: "No - my grandfather's"

    Sergeant: "Does he know you are using it?"

    Answer: "No - I think he is inspecting Tibet; but he has left it with us."

    There was a pause, while he digested my answer that my grandfather was "inspecting Tibet".

    Sergeant: "I see; but do you know that the Ministerial flag can only be flown if your grandfather is in the car."

    Answer: "Yes; I am very sorry".

    Sergeant: "That is not enough; your driver could be arrested, even you perhaps, but you are under age. Did you know that every policeman in Punjab, let alone Lahore, knows whose car this is?"

    Answer: "Yes."

Sergeant: "Shall I report to your father and/or your grandfather?"

Answer: "Please, no."

Sergeant: "This is the first time you have said 'please'. Get out of the car, and furl and sheate the flag."

Answer: "But the driver is outside, he can do it."

Sergeant: "You will do what I say; get out and do it yourself. Nothing more will be said, and don't do it again."

It was another lesson in humility. My father did find out, but not, I think, my grandfather.

Lahore was also the place for my first educational institution. Until the age of 8, my two younger sisters and I were educated at home. I think there was more than one tutor - one for English, one for Maths, and possibly a third for things like geography etc, while my sisters had a lady to teach them music. They were kind and instructive and I remember them with affection to this day. But my first school was the Joan MacDonald Prep School in Lahore. Run and jointly owned by a kind Scottish lady, and a dragon of an Indian Christian lady called Miss Singha (meaning appropriately "Lion"), it was a happy day school. It was where I first experienced a sensation that any red blooded male experiences in the process of growing up. One of my teachers was a Miss Pant, pronounced "Punth". (Her sister later married the assassinated first Prime Minister of Pakistan, Nawab Liaqat Ali.) She was beautiful, taught me English, but also showed us yoga exercises. Looking at her during them was when I first felt the vague glimmerings of sexual desire, without realising what it was I felt. Much to my delight, she frequently singled me out for praise, and everyone felt I was her favourite pupil - I may have been then, but years later, it was 1977 I think, when I was much in the news in England and in India, I met her again at a dinner party in Delhi. She had married a very rich businessman, and at her house where a friend took me, she said she was delighted to meet me, had been reading all about me, and how nice etc. to meet the first Asian Tory Party Candidate of this century etc. etc.

I said: "But don't you remember me?"

"Yes, of course, I should; Lahore, Lucknow or Simla?"

"Lahore."

"I am trying hard to remember you."

"But I always thought I was your favourite pupil."

This female fickleness was certainly a blow to my ego.

Life in Simla moved at an even gentler pace than in Lahore. It was not only the summer capital, but also where many non-official families moved up for the summer. All the Punjab Princes had residences there, and there was much fun and gaiety; but those who wanted a "fast" time" preferred the other hill station of Mussorie, which did not have the Viceregal presence restraining untoward behaviour. Many of the princes from other parts of India went to Mussorie, where their peccadilloes would not so easily come to the notice of the Viceroy, and therefore to the Secretary of State for India in London. Some princely states were the size of Wales, but a number were very small, like Bhajji a few miles from Simla. The Young Raja, Rampal, was a contemporary at school, and I saw him riding one day, followed by a policeman from his state, which really only had two policemen in all.

"Where is the other policeman?" I asked.

"Guarding the palace in case of revolution," was the Raja's answer.

3
Education

I think it was Sir Osbert Sitwell, in his entry in *Who's Who*, who stated that he was 'educated during the holidays from Eton'. I used to laugh about this with his nephew and heir, Sir Reresby Sitwell, and of course it depends on what one means by the word education. I think it is not just turning oneself literate, which is obviously the basis of it. Neither is it merely to acquire skills to be able to find employment, which appears to be the modern emphasis. Next to the Spirit in oneself, the mind is our governing agent, and surely the purpose of education should be to broaden and enrich it, to develop its faculty to question and find answers, and having found a few – for nobody can find all – to continue to question. Education should therefore be broad based, it should teach the mind how to stretch itself so that when the phase of formal education is over, it continues to do so. Skills that are taught with the purpose of merely finding bread and butter do not always necessarily benefit the mind. I recall one evening in Greenwich when I was its Parliamentary Candidate, and a kind supporter had asked my wife and I to dinner along with a few fellow Tory supporters and also one or two other couples who could be described as 'wobblers'. It was no surprise that the wife in the case of one pair was a teacher, and left wing at that. In the free ranging discussion that evening, the subject came around to education and the inevitable argument about the private and public sector. I have always supported the principle of universal education, but also that it should be of the highest quality possible, to encourage and nurture all who are talented, and not to be mediocre or even sub standard, holding back the intelligent and hard working in order to keep pace with the lowest common denominator amongst their classmates. The teaching profession in the United Kingdom has a great deal to answer for to the generations since the 1960's, which it has taught and left ill equipped to fight their way through the world. If these generations of teachers were and are genuinely well intentioned, their consciences should be troubling them greatly at what they have done. On the other hand, if their practices result from mere ideology, they must view with satisfaction the numbers they have so ill educated that not only have they succeeded in creating an underclass, but the gap is getting ever wider between the well educated and those not so. With increasing technology and speed of communication, this would of course make it much easier for future local Stalins to control the proletariat in Western societies. George Orwell's 1984 does not now appear as a nightmare, but as a probability.

However, this was more or less the range of conversation that evening. The lady teacher was naturally quite vehement and vociferous about her point of view and equality and so on. I asked her whether equality had ever existed, and whether it ever could. In my view, the only equality that can be found anywhere is in mathematics, where zero equals zero. In no other case in the whole universe can equality be found, not in nature, animal, plant or the human world. Everything and everyone is uniquely and interestingly different, the reasons for which are known only to our Creator.

She bridled, and asked me what I then thought was the purpose of education. 'Taking one criterion', I replied 'if it is accepted that the general state of humankind in unhappiness, the purpose of education should or must be to teach the mind to choose its branch of unhappiness'. Her husband who was undoubtedly henpecked looked at her with such glee, and said, 'Come on, you are a teacher; have you ever thought of that?' I fear I lost her vote that night, but consoled myself that I'd probably secured the husband's!

Whatever the other misfortunes in my life, my brothers and sisters were fortunate in the education planned and provided by our parents. There were only sixteen months between me and my next sibling, a sister called Raj. Apart from education at home, we were sent to Joan McDonald's Prep School at about the same time. I remember well those mornings in Lahore during the winter months, where the Punjab winter could be fiercely cold – the summer months were always in Simla – being woken up early by the servants, dressed and then breakfast where our maternal grandmother would invariably supervise that we ate well. She always insisted that we had almonds, even more so on days of tests and examinations because they are supposed to be good for the brain. After breakfast, the chauffeur Bhopal Singh would drive us the two miles or so to school, which was on a road called the Lower Mall, at the end of which lay the impressive buildings of the Punjab Secretariat, the seat of power, administration and authority for the Province, and also my father's office. Somewhere late in the course of the morning, in our separate classes Raj and I would have the comforting and reassuring sight of our father being driven to his office around 10 a.m. There would be two more sightings of Bhopal Singh during the day when he brought our lunch, and when he picked us up after school ended. We could eat our lunch, either at our desks, or sitting in the car, or make a picnic of it under a tree; boys and girls either brought it with them, or their households sent it to them, as in our case. Our luncheon basket and tiffin carrier were a joy to look forward to, wondering what our beloved cook, Bachan Singh had sent us that day. He had a wide repertoire of dishes, Indian and English, and the only time I tried to resist his blandishments was when he served me fish cakes. It should be remembered that the Punjab is approximately six hundred miles from the sea, so that fish is comparatively strange to us. The local fish was from the Ravi river, one of the five mighty rivers rising in the Himalayas and flowing into the Arabian Sea. I would like to digress a little here. I have always loved what rude friends have described as 'useless information'. My head is full of it. If you stand on the tip of Cape Comorin, the southern most tip of the Indian subcontinent there is nothing but water until the Antarctic continent, equally so if you stand under an umbrella on the high point of Jakhoo Hill in Simla facing north, in the rainy season, the drop of rain falling off your umbrella on the left hand side will end up in the Arabian Sea, while those on the right will end up on the Bay of Bengal. That particular point in Simla is a perfect watershed. Water draining away to the left goes into the Sutlej, one of the five Punjab rivers, and that on the right drains into the Ganges flowing into the Bay of Bengal.

Apart from the basic three R's which we were taught well, I can't really remember what other subjects, if any, there were. I think I must have been 9 years or so old when I was admitted to St Anthony's School as a day boy. This was run by a team of Irish Lay Brothers, and had a established reputation for firm discipline and high academic achievement. My father had planned that after a few years here, I would go to Aitchison Chiefs' College, of which more later. Because of the War, petrol rationing had by then been introduced and there was therefore little question of being driven to school and back. The car was now mainly used to and from the office by my father, and occasionally by my mother for brief outings or shopping trips. Such shopping was, of course, minimal. All household requirements were organised by the servants, and for a lot of other goods the merchants used to visit the house and display them on our verandah, for my mother to pick and choose. As an alternative method of transport, my father purchased a Victoria (a sort of landau named after the former Queen Empress, pulled by only one horse). It was a handsome affair, and the servants always wanted the horse to be gaily caparisoned almost to the point of vulgarity. However, by now I was the proud owner of a spanking new Raleigh bicycle, which I used every day to ride the three miles or so each way to St Anthony's School. Apart from a few bicycles and tongas (horse pulled 4 seater contraptions plying for hire) there was little traffic, practically no cars or other vehicles and it was a joy to cycle each morning and afternoon.

The teaching standards and standards expected of the pupils at St Anthony's were very high indeed. Apart from English Language and Literature, I was immediately launched into Algebra, Geometry, Physics, Chemistry, English History and Geography. Sadly there was no Greek, Latin or foreign language taught then, but I did take Urdu as one of my subjects. When spoken it is not vastly different from Hindustani, the lingua franca of Northern India; but it is written in the Arabic script, from right to left. It is an amalgam of Persian, Arabic, a smattering of Turkish and of course Hindustani. It was generated and grew in the early days of the Moghul Empire as a linguistic bridge between the Court which spoke mainly Persian, and its Army and other subjects. I still remember the names of the Irish brothers, Gannon, Henderson and Ritchie - always addressed as 'Brother' by the pupils – who taught English, History and Geography. Mathematics was taught by a Mr Price – always addressed as 'Sir' – who was a strict disciplinarian not hesitating to cane the errant. I was beaten a number of times in my five years at St Anthony's, often for minor misdemeanours like getting a sum wrong. The standard punishment ranged from 1 stroke to 6, with the choice of having it on your palm or your bottom. Wherever it was, it was pretty painful during and for some time after. However, I don't think any of us bore any serious grudges for being beaten, or as in my case lessen the affection and respect I felt for the brothers, and Masters like Mr Price. Physics and Chemistry were taught by an Indian Master, Mr Sharma. I enjoyed my studies, the tests and examinations and if the thought had even occurred to me, could well have tried to become an academic. Although for a short period I toyed with Advanced Mathematics like trigonometry, I was not as good in Mathematics and Science as I was in other subjects. For our School Certificate – the then equivalent of 'O' levels – we did the Tudor period in English History, and books like Boswell's *Johnson* and *Silas*

Marner by George Eliot. I can still recall a lot of these, but little of Chemistry except for the laboratory with it Bunsen burners and various alkaline solutions, little of Physics except for the speed of light and sound etc; however I do remember almost all the geometrical theorems, particularly Pythagoras. We sat our School Certificate Examination not in St Anthony's, but in hall provided by the Punjab University, quite near my earlier school and father's office. The hall was vast, because there were pupils from several other schools also taking the exams. I think the whole affair lasted about four or five days, with different papers being taken mornings and afternoons, sometimes even two in the course of half a day. Things were certainly not made easy for us. One morning we could do Arithmetic and History tests, in the same afternoon English Literature and Physics; there were no convenience aids like calculators. The word 'numerate' was hardly ever used at the time, but we were certainly numerate because we had to do everything in our heads, providing me with a lifelong advantage – I find I can still do things as quickly as ever or even quicker while somebody else is wrestling with his or her calculator. It is ironical that there are probably fewer people who are numerate now when the word is in common use, than there were when it was hardly used, almost unknown. Use of the car was restored to me for the duration of the exams, with Bhopal again bringing my lunch – breakfast having been very early with a preponderance of salted, fried or roasted almonds and my grandmother at table with me, almost feeding me and stiffening my morale and resolve.

We would not know the exam results for at least three months – being the Cambridge School Certificate, our papers were always sent to England to be marked; being the War, they went by ship around the Cape of Good Hope thereby taking around six weeks in each direction. On one or two occasions the ship concerned was sunk by enemy action. The powers that be had thought of that – our answers were written out in duplicate, with my first experience of using carbon paper. I blush with modesty in mentioning my results. No actual marks were allocated, but your results in each paper were graded in descending order – 'A' or Distinction if you got more than 75%, 'C' or Credit for marks between 65–75%, 'P' or Pass between 50% and 60%, and 'F' or Failed below 50%. I obtained an 'A' in English Language, Literature, History, Geography and Arithmetic; 'C' in Algebra, Geometry, Physics, and Chemistry.

After this, the time had come to go on to my final school, Aitchison, also in Lahore. It was founded in 1886 by Sir Charles Aitchison, then Lt Governor of the Punjab, with the purpose of educating the Punjab Princes, nobility and aristocracy on English public school lines. Wags used to say 'to also keep us out of mischief and from plotting against the British'. The Punjab was the last territory to fall to the British in what eventually became British India – it should be remembered that the rest of India remained Princely India, and it was much larger than British territory, consisting of several States independent of the British in everything except Defence, Foreign Policy and rail transport. The largest of these States were larger than the size of Wales, the smallest probably no bigger than Green Park in London. Apart from Kashmir with a Hindu ruler, there were five large States in Northern India with Sikh rulers viz. Patiala, Nabha, Jind, Kapurthala and Faridkot, the first three of which were ruled by dynasties of a common ancestry. There was one small State with a Muslim ruler, Maler Kotla, but Aitchison College also had boys from the ruling families of two large Muslim States in Sind, Bahawalpur and Khairpur. Except for Kashmir which was a post East India Company creation, all the other States pre-dated the British in India, although were nowhere as old as the Rajput States, some of which go back to antiquity.

The nobility and aristocracy in the Punjab were mainly Muslim, followed by a number of Sikh families. The very wealthy Hindu families in the Punjab were not aristocratic or noble, their wealth not being based on land; however their boys were eligible for admission to Aitchison. Eligibility was restricted to those families who were mentioned in the 'Golden Book of India', a rather unsophisticated version of Debrett's or Burke's. The school was unashamedly exclusive – the word 'elitist' had not been invented, not that anyone would have cared a fig even if it had been in usage. We would have sport fixtures only against equal institutions e.g. Mayo Chiefs' College, which educated the Rajput royalty and nobility. Therefore we did not play cricket (at which we were particularly good) against any other team in Lahore with its numerous places of education, except for the Governor's Eleven who were deemed fit but only just. We took to the extreme the principle of amateurs, being gentlemen, hardly ever playing against professionals. We did not play even most amateurs.

The last issue of the school magazine in 1946 – before the destructive changes brought about by the Transfer of Power in 1947 – includes the speech given by the then Viceroy, Lord Curzon at the school prize giving in April 1899. The scheme of reorganisation which was soon adopted by the College owed its inception to Curzon himself. Extracts of his speech are quoted below.

'Aitchison College has not been founded in our interests. It is not a device that has been constructed by the Government in order to bring either credit or advantage to the British Raj. It is an institution that has been founded in your interests, in the interests of your families and fortunes, and your Province. You ought, therefore, Chiefs of the Punjab, to give this College greater support than you have hitherto done.

Believe me, the days are gone by when the hereditary aristocracy, however noble its origin or however illustrious its service, can sit still with folded hands and contemplate the glories of the past. If you are to hold your own in the estates which you enjoy by virtue of your position, and win the confidence of your people, you must come forth from your isolation, and show that you are fitted with character and worth for the position which everyone is ready to conceded to you. You must march alongside of knowledge, instead of toiling hopelessly and feebly behind it; you must reinforce the claims of your birth by equally high attainments. You must realise above all, that destiny is not a passive influence that lies in the laps of the Gods, but it is an active instrument that is in your own hands to shape as you will. In the years that lie ahead the Punjab and the princely States will need men deeply influenced by a spirit of service – rulers, landlords, Ministers, politicians, farmers engineers ...

The need will be for men who have been educated in mind, body and spirit, and not in mind alone; for education is not an achievement of the brain alone, but a co-ordination of mind, body and spirit. It should foster a sense and spirit of responsibility, an idea of service, and a healthy independence which has learnt the value of self-help. The Punjab and the States will need men who have acquired the benefits of western civilisation without losing the heritage of their birth.'

Lord Curzon was making some telling points in his speech. When the school was founded in 1882 as 'a place for the young nobility of the Punjab', subscriptions were called for from the ruling Princes. It was these contributions which made the foundation of the College possible. One Prince sent a generous donation on the tacit understanding that it would relieve him from the unpleasant obligation of sending his sons and relatives to the College. Once, however, the advantages of the College were realised, including the comfortable accommodation it offered in Lahore, the capital of the Province, there was little reluctance to be entered for the College. In fact, until after the First World War, some boys continued to live there until they were 21 years old. I should have mentioned that they all brought their own retinue of servants with them, and had their own kitchens. In my time in the 1940's, we were restricted to one personal servant each, in addition to the servants provided by the institution, including grooms for our riding school and stables; but no separate kitchens were allowed, and we ate communally in each House, the fare invariably being good or better supplemented by an excellent tuck shop. Amusingly enough, during my time there, one boy did indeed remain on at the College while well past the usual school leaving age – he was finally persuaded to leave around the age of 22. Born to greatness as the Khan of

Bugt and ruler of a large swathe of Baluchistan, he continues to play at the time of writing, a prominent part in the political life of Pakistan, being only narrowly defeated in 1994 for the presidency of the country.

The same issue of the magazine contains old boys News, and the names of those honoured in the king Emperor's Birthday Honours List, 1946. These names include Their Highnesses The Maharajdhiraj of Patiala, the Raja of Mandi, the Raja of Faridkot, the Hon Sir Firoz Khan Noon, Malik Ahmed Yar Tiwana and so on. This was more or less the ethos in which I had the pleasure and privilege to be formed and to mature.

Floreat Aitchisonia

At Aitchison, there were houses named after former Housemasters, Kelly and Godley; there was also Leslie-Jones House for day boys, and during the War we had a house called Churchill House for English boys evacuated from schools like Eton and Harrow and others in England, as also English boys in India prevented by the War from being sent to England for their education. Boys were accommodated, fed and all manners of necessary administration were within their respective House system. Additionally, because some Rulers might have a number of sons at school at the same time – all of them of course from different mothers – they had their own house for accommodation and messing e.g. Bhawalpur House. All these were in the school grounds, which also included our riding school, swimming pool, separate places of worship for Hindu, Muslim and Sikh boys, an excellent modern block called the Science Block with the latest teaching aids for science subjects, a hospital, several acres of farmland – we grew our own wheat, vegetables etc, and along with the dairy were almost self sufficient in food – and of course vast playing fields for cricket, hockey etc. These playing fields so impressed HM King George V when he visited Aitchison in 1911 during his itinerary for the Imperial Durbar, that he commented:. "My God, this beats Eton any time."

The hub of the whole College was the Old Building built in the late 1880's or early 1890s in the Indian Saracenic style which had become fashionable in India during the days of the Moghul Empire. It is now a preserved building in Pakistan, equivalent to a Grade I listing in our towns in England. Apparently, apart from the Mosque in Lahore, and the Emperor Jehangir's mausoleum a few miles away on the banks of the river Ravi, there are no other historical buildings in Pakistan. The reason, of course, is that the Moghul dynasty, and preceding Empires in India, always had Delhi or Agra as their imperial capital, and these were 312 miles further east, with even older buildings in the Rajput states which are another hundreds of miles further south east. The College Old Building had the offices of the Principal and Headmaster (we had both), the School Assembly Hall and two or three small classrooms for the senior boys, like myself studying for the Cambridge Higher School Certificate or the equivalent of the current 'A' levels; if I recall correctly, there were only about eight to ten boys in the senior school, divided into two groups of four or five each, i.e. those studying Science or Arts. I was one of the latter, and my subjects were History, (Stuart period), English Literature (mainly Shakespeare), Constitutional History, Economics and Geography. Our classrooms held only 4 to 5 desks, so that it was an excellent teacher/pupil ratio. In the Arts section apart from myself there was young Younis Sadiq (later to achieve modest fame in a war film as a pilot in the RAF raid on the heavy water plant in Norway), Maharajkumar Kirininder Singh, a younger brother of the Maharaja of Patiala (in all he had 86 brothers and sisters), Atam Dev the wealthiest Hindu landowner in the Punjab and Nawabzada Mubarak Ali Khan, seventeenth son of the Nawab of Bhawalpur. His desk was next to mine, and almost daily when the opportunity arose he would put on his desk a list of 17 names starting with his father, the Nawab. I would then hear him mumbling to himself, and crossing off the names on the list. 'The old boy will die soon,' he would mumble, 'the heir apparent could be made to die in a polo accident, the next chap could be poisoned' and so on until he would finish the exercise by saying, 'And now I shall be the Nawab'. This was an early preview therefore of that excellent film with Alec Guinness taking seven parts in "Kind Hearts and Coronets". Victor Kiernan taught us History – he was an odd choice to be a master at Aitchison because we all knew he was Communist; in any case, he taught well and he was well liked. A Miss Loveday Prior taught us English Literature (her brother was a General, and then Resident of the Rajputana States); and Mr J C Luther (who later joined the Civil Service and rose to become the Deputy Governor of the Reserve Bank of India, the Indian counterpart of the Bank of England) was the Master for Economics, Political Constitution, Geography and any other miscellaneous subjects.

I think the day started with the School Assembly at 8 a.m., to which we would cycle the quarter mile or so from our House, then cycling back for breakfast through our lovely school grounds full of colourful flowerbeds and oleander blossom and gul mohar trees. Then it would be back to the Old Building for four or five classes until lunch time with a 20 minute break in between when we would cycle furiously to the tuck shop where each of us had an account eventually reflected in the term's bill sent to one's father, guardian or relevant Princely States Treasurer, as the case may be. I don't think there were any classes after lunch, the afternoon being entirely taken up by games, swimming or riding. There was no compulsory prep, and as senior boys we had the freedom to leave the school grounds outside school hours, but be back by 10 p.m. All that was required was to enter details in the Signing Out Book about where one was going. This was an early manifestation of security, but it was necessary. Considering the type of student at Aitchison, there was concern that there might be unpleasantness in Lahore with communists or protagonists agitating for the British to quit India. This never happened as I remember, but the CID and other relevant authorities were alerted daily to the whereabouts of the more important boys. Since my family lived in Lahore, my address was often quoted in the Signing Out Book, with one or the other of my companions writing in 'Gone off to visit/invited by Saroop's parents'. Of course this couldn't last. Our Housemaster was impressed and puzzled by the frequency with which boys in his house were being entertained by my family, sometimes on evenings when I myself was in the school. He didn't say anything, but one evening he telephoned my parents to en-quire about one boy who had employed this stratagem on that day. My father was not available, so the servants connected him to my mother, who replied blithely that she loved entertaining my friends, but it was a long time since any of them had come. In the civilised, gentle ways of Aitchison, there was no chastisement of the culprits, but a huge notice soon appeared adjacent to the 'Signing Out Book'. It read 'Boys being entertained by Saroop's parents will henceforth have to produce a written invitation'.

There were, again, only around seven of us boarding in our House, known as Bungalow No 2, No 1 being the Headmaster's residence – an enormous place with a lovely garden and lawn. Each of us had our own personal servant, who organised everything for his master, including waiting at table. My own was called Inder, a cheerful, clean fellow only a few years older than myself, who had been specially chosen by my mother to accompany me. His father had worked for us before him, and I lost track of him when I later went off to join the Indian Military Academy. My mother told me that he was one of the staff who had to go after 1947, when we couldn't afford to keep them all – the partition of India provided a most serious blow to our family's fortunes. Walking on the Mall in the 1950's with my mother, we came across him doing manual labour as a rickshaw puller. We fell on each other's shoulders, and he started crying and saying how comfortable he had been as a member of 'our family'.

We had a room and bathroom each to our selves, with a com-mon drawing room and a dining room. The food was good, but in any case could always be supplemented from outside. There was technical limit of a £5.00 equivalent per month as pocket money (probably over £100.00 in today's terms) but this was not strictly adhered to. I can honestly say that I have never been so carefree or comfortably off, with a servant and motorcycle all paid for by my father. I used to fill up with petrol at the pump where we had an account. I don't know why the other senior boys did not keep cars – some of them could easily have afforded a Rolls. I could use it only outside school hours, and was naturally popular in providing lifts. I remember two incidents particularly. One afternoon, our Economics Master Mr Luther, asked me if he could try it. He had never ridden one before, so I showed him how to start it, gears etc. I genuinely forgot to tell him how to stop it, and he forgot to ask. We therefore had the sight of him going over all the school roads and paths, and shouting every time he passed me 'Narindar, how do I stop it?'. Eventually, the petrol ran out as there had not been much in the tank; there were no hard feelings on his part, but my popularity soared in the school where everyone thought I had played a good practical joke. The second incident occurred in my last term at Aitchison, just before I left for the Indian Military Academy. By then I had discovered the charms of female company, and was squiring around a most attractive girl called Wendy Boswell who was some years older and had served in WACI's (Womens' Auxiliary Corps of India – equivalent of the English ATS). She was obviously using me, if only to fill in time between her other more mature and interesting admirers. My motorcycle did not have a proper pillion, and I did not know that having a passenger without it was breaking the law. We were spinning down the Mall, virtually traffic free in those days, with the thrill of speed and her arms around me, when I was stopped by an over zealous policeman. Rather crossly, I told him I was not aware that I was doing anything wrong, and that if he persisted in taking the matter further he would be the loser. During this discussion, a police sergeant drew up alongside on his Harley Davidson. I was worried if he might be the same as in the incident a few years earlier over flying my grandfather's flag, although he wasn't. He told me he had to stop our discussion, and told the policeman to drop the matter, 'and that is an order'. We shot off, and I shouted to Wendy over the wind 'He must have known I am at Aitchison, and therefore not easy to prosecute'. She laughed and said 'You idiot, that was my father'.

The pace of academic life was gentle. Aitchison broke up in Lahore for the summer holidays, in mid April, and we did not return until towards end September. During this period, a skeleton teaching staff moved up to an enormous house in the hills in Simla, where most of us would in any case be spending our summer holidays. Those who so wished could go to the classes in the temporary school, but it was not compulsory. Lahore starts to get very hot from mid April onwards, but the period between early March and then used to be very pleasant, a short spring. A tradition had evolved that in March/April when the weather was warming up, if we had a cloudy or showery day, the whole school would adjourn the few miles to the banks of the Ravi river, and classes conducted there. This was great fun, more like a picnic with the House kitchens also transported to provide lunch for young, hungry boys, appetites whetted by the proximity of the river (about half a mile wide at that point) and the excitement of it all. But, of course, some were never satisfied. My classmate, Atam Dev, used to grumble that there was no point at all in studying if the temperature was above 75°F; the whole school should close down much earlier for the summer holidays.

I took two extra subjects, at additional cost to my poor father; piano lessons and French, but this was only in my last term. A dear Austrian lady who taught music in the junior school gallantly undertook to teach me to no avail. Much as I love music, I just do not have musical skills; for the life of me I could not learn to read the music sheets. All I remember is what an octave is. Success in French was equally difficult to achieve partly because I didn't take it seriously enough, and partly because of distractions. My tutor in French, who had only recently joined Aitchison, was Alex Milne, a genial Scot who had been in the Colonial Service in Malaya followed by a stint in King Edward VII's own Gurkha Rifles. He was a fluent linguist, and I used to go to his home three evenings a week for my lessons. He shared a bungalow with Miss Prior, a grand handsome lady, brother a general, and from a line of Empire men; in reality the house was divided into two. Miss Prior used to drop in from time to time, as she had always evinced platonic affection for me.

One evening when she dropped in, she found a few other senior boys there, including one old boy the Khan of Bugti who used to come and stay in his old school for weeks on end as a change from his vast dusty fiefdom in Baluchistan. We were about to leave, and were slightly embarrassed to be asked where we were going by Miss Prior. The Khan had invited all of us to dinner, including Milne, at a marvellous restaurant cum night club called Stiffles run by a White Russian Émigré. Lahore had four or five such establishments, each with splendid food and some of India's finest bands. Rudy Cotton at Stiffles was in the Joe Loss class, and the whole atmosphere was rather like the old 400 Club in Leicester Square. Since Alex Milne was with us, the deadline of 10 p.m. back at school did not apply. We got pleasantly inebriated, and after a delicious meal, Bugti said ' Boys, I've got a surprise for you', with Alex saying 'Your education will continue tonight'.

Bugti was taking us to Lahore's red light district known as Hira Mandi which translates as the Market of Diamonds. When our taxis dropped us there, word immediately got around that Chiefs' College boys were there, and prices shot up in all streets in the district. I have very hazy, or little, recollections about the rest of the night. I remember getting back to Milne's house, and flopping down on the sofa. Sometime later I woke to the sound of him playing the piano, stark naked and singing at the top of his voice. I fell back into a drunken stupor, but in the morning made my way back to my room, breakfasted and was in class, not feeling very bright. I sensed something strange in the atmosphere; my classmates were grinning at me, one or two winked, and the master taking the class, J Luther looked at me in a peculiar way – that class should have been taken by Miss Prior, but had been switched. I was soon to find out why.

A little later a uniformed flunkey came into the classroom, and said that my presence was required in the office of the Headmaster, Mr Ward. I should have mentioned him earlier – of benign mien, backed by an equally kind disposition. He had also recently become engaged to Miss Prior. As I walked through the outer office containing his clerical staff who also gave me strange looks, I felt a sense of impending doom. I was right. The Head was kind, asked me to sit down, and to tell him absolutely truthfully about what had happened last night. I did, exactly as I remembered it. He was a silent for awhile, and then said 'Narindar, I believe you, but I had feared something worse. Nevertheless, you have not behaved well. I shall be writing to your father telling him that if this was not your last term, we would have to ask him to withdraw you'. At lunch, I became acquainted with the rumour going round like bushfire throughout the school. I was being looked on for reasons which were false and which I didn't like. But it was too late, since all believed that Miss Prior had been woken by Alex's caterwauling, walked in to chastise him, screamed when she saw him naked and he had been abusive in return; that afterwards if not him, I had forced my attentions upon her. The last bit was totally untrue, and the first bit I must have slept through. However, Aitchison had not had such a salacious incident since the days in the late 1920s when boys used to entertain courtesans in their room, and any master passing by was invited to join in. Milne left, and took up employment as the governor and tutor to the Yuvraj (heir apparent) of Faridkot. Years later I heard he had settled in Bugti as a sort of permanent guest of the Khan's. He was one of those amusing, individualistic and talented Empire men who find average life dull beyond words, and who can blame them. With characteristic generosity, neither Ward or Miss Prior held much against me, and it gave me great joy when I ran into them a few months later at the Gaiety Theatre in Simla. I greeted her as 'Mrs Ward', she snappped open her fan, kissed me on the cheek and said "Clever boy"; the first Aitchisonian to call me that'.

So I left Aitchison in an unwanted blaze of glory as far as the boys were concerned, but in some disgrace with the authorities. My days there, indeed all my schooldays, were happy ones. It puzzles me when I hear so many people saying how much they hated their time at public school. Of course, Aitchison was most unusual, and little did I realise then that some of the happiest years of my life were over. Ahead lay many rocky ones, full of what nowadays would be called stress, at times to overflowing levels.

I always think of Aitchison with great affection and gratitude, and felt most honoured in the 1980s when I was elected President of the Old Boys Association.

Floreat Aitchisonia!

4
The Dreadful Watershed
of 1947

Little did I realise when I left Aitchison what a sheltered world I was leaving; at home a flat for myself was built as an extension to our main residence in Lahore when I was 14 years old because I had complained strongly about lack of privacy and quiet with the antics and noise of my six siblings in the big house; a personal servant was there and later on at school; no worries of any kind, even exams which I loved. From here onwards I was to feel the cold winds of life, and to learn at an early enough age to deal with reality – not so much to adapt because I have never been very good at that, but to do your best and damnedest to get reality to adapt to yourself, even to a miniscule degree.

The transfer of power in 1947 took most by surprise by the rapidity with which it was announced and implemented. Enough, or probably not enough, has been written about it. It caused untold misery, caused more havoc and deaths than have even been near enough estimated. In 1954, when my then wife and I were spending a weekend at the Mountbatten estate, Broadlands, the subject came up, and Lord Mountbatten was, quite correctly from his point of view, rather cross about it. 'I have saved more lives than I might have been responsible for getting killed'. Later that evening when we were going off to bed, his younger daughter Lady Pamela Hicks, (a friend of my wife's and that is why we had been invited for the weekend) said 'Don't worry; but he is terribly sensitive on that subject'.

Historians and analysts have debated, and will continue to debate the subject. All I can say from the average Indian point of view is that nobody, but nobody, wanted freedom at that price. Gandhi had publicly stated that even if it meant chaos and bad rule, it was better than being under foreign rule. He soon found his words haunting him. To his credit, he was against Partition to the end, as were a number of leading and sensible nationalists like Rajagopalachari who a year later became the first and only Indian Governor General. It was the other leading politicians in the two leading parties, viz. the Congress and the Muslim League, people like Nehru, Jinnah and Patel who were hungry for power, who realised that they were getting old and that it might pass them by, who successfully agitated for the British to leave sooner than they need or should have done.

The Punjab was the key to Jinnah's dream of Pakistan; without the Punjab it was hollow. Since the mid 1920s until 1946 the province had been governed by the Unionist Party, of which my grandfather was a co-founder. It was rightly called such because it united the Muslims (who were the majority in the province), the Sikhs and the Hindus. Its axiom, propagated by my grandfather, was that religion should not come into politics. The Punjab was considered the best administered province in the whole country, probably in the Empire, and in the words of Lord Linlithgow, Viceroy of India from 1935 to 1943, "The Punjab was a dream". The Unionist Party was elected to power, election after election, trouncing the Congress and Muslim League. It was not collaborationist, as vilified by its detractors, but realistic. I remember my grandfather saying that of course the British would have to go one day, but not until we had put our own house in order. He put their departure date at around 1960 – if that had really happened, the winds of change in Africa would have been towards the late '70s, and the map of the world, and regional balances of power could well have been different from those today.

He also disagreed with Gandhi on the principle of non-cooperation with the British during the War. Whereas Congress ministries in seven out of eleven Indian provinces resigned at the outbreak of World War II (thus denying themselves the opportunity and experience of governing, the lack of which was to cost India dearly in all years to now since 1947), the Punjab stood firm. On that day, my grandfather made a historic public announcement, 'If England fights, the Punjab fights alongside'. As far as I know no annals of the period record what I learnt years later from Sir Khizar Hayat Tiwana, the last Premier (as they were officially called to distinguish them from the Prime Minister in Downing Street) of undivided Punjab. In 1941 his predecessor, Sir Sikander Hayat went to the Middle East and North Africa to show the home flag to the thousands of Indian troops fighting in those theatres of war. He had a meeting with Sir Winston Churchill and Field Marshal Smuts in Cairo. Knowing he had the full backing of my grandfather he said words to the effect, 'Prime Minister, we all know that the British will leave some time after the War is over. Please leave the Punjab alone, but give us an outlet to the sea '(Karachi would have been the only choice); 'we have no minerals or other resources, but we are self sufficient in food and hard working. Also, let us agree to settle our demobilised soldiers in Mesopotamia, they are farmers and will turn the area green, and with the added advantage that in that sensitive part of the world, Britain will have a pro-British presence'. This would have obviously appealed to Churchill's romantic frame of mind. 'Partition India', he said, 'over my dead body; but if so the Punjab will be treated as a special case'.

When recounting this to me in 1974 a few months before he died, Sir Khizar told me that he owed his Premiership to my grandfather. Early in 1942 Sir Sikandar died; Punjab Assembly, its Governor Sir Bertrand Glancy and the Viceroy Lord Linlithgow wanted my grandfather to succeed him; but he said: "No, the Punjab is a Muslim majority province, its Premier should be a Muslim," and he backed Sir Khizar. The latter continued to tell me that he knew when Labour won the General Election in 1945, it was all over. They would countenance Partition in their haste to hand over power. Sir Khizar gamely carried on, with both the Congress and Muslim League harrying him in the legislature, and rumblings outside of the civil disorder and chaos that were to come. In 1946 while attending the Paris Peace Conference as one of India's delegates, he resigned, not to return to the Indian sub-continent until the early 1950s. Amongst the papers he left me is the passenger list of one of the trans-Atlantic crossings of the Queen Mary. In that most distinguished list, only two names are shown as travelling each with a valet – Sir Winston and Lady Churchill and Sir Khizar and Lady Tiwana. He saw Sir Winston regularly until he died in 1965, and continued to call on Lady Churchill afterwards. With the break-up of the Unionist Government, the Punjab began to slide into chaos, and the period from March 1947 onwards indicated the communal blood bath that was to follow later. There is plenty written about that elsewhere.

Our own departure for Simla that summer was so different from the preceding 14 years of the annual migration to the hills. My father asked me to take one of our two cars with one servant; he, the rest of the family (five siblings at the time) with the rest of the staff would follow by train. One car and my motorbike were left behind, the car never to be seen again, but my motorcycle and some of our belongings were rescued by my father two years later when he went back to Lahore, then in Pakistan, with a military escort. By the time they left Lahore was a dangerous place. Mobs, mostly a violent version of Rent a Crowd were on the rampage, killing and looting indiscriminately. Civil power had broken down, and even the recently imposed martial law was unable to prevent atrocities taking place. On their way to the railway station, the family were joined by my father's Muslim Private Secretary, Mohammad Aslam, loyal and stout to the last, even though my father had forbidden him. On the platform he insisted on being on the train until Amritsar, where Hindu and Sikh majority areas began, thus offering some safety; but he would have to run the gauntlet twice, including the return journey. 'You have always carried out my orders; you will carry out this last one; you are not to come', said my father. They parted in tears, and although both survived, were not destined to see each other again.

We all met up in Simla; I had an uneventful journey except for the petrol shortage. One could only buy petrol with an authorisation paper from the local Deputy Commissioner or Superintendent of Police, administrative and police heads respectively of each district. I required this at two points during the 300 mile drive, but this was no hardship in those days, everyone knew everyone else. Settling down in Simla was a gloomy affair. Although mid August had been announced as the date for the transfer of power, the boundaries of the two new Dominions, India and Pakistan, had not yet been fixed. Sir Cyril Radcliffe, an English lawyer who had never before been to India was toiling away on this in the heat of Delhi. We didn't know whether Lahore would finally lie in India or in Pakistan, and it was obvious that as non-Muslims we couldn't return if it were in the latter, as it shortly turned out to be.

As the eldest child, now mature, I was soon informed by my parents about the predicament the family was in – the other children did not know, neither did the servants as yet. We had no money, literally no money. There was no income coming in either from landed or urban property now in Pakistan. The bank accounts holding whatever cash we had were also there. Not that we were ever in that category, but the landed classes in the Punjab never did have any foreign accounts in Switzerland, or property in the South of France; it wouldn't have occurred to us to take any money out of India; the lands we possessed had been taken by the sword or were granted as a reward for service by the sword. It was all taken away by a stroke of the pen. Until things were restored to some balance about a year later, the family lived firstly on credit which was good with all the suppliers in Simla who knew us well, the one deserving mention would be the local Fortnum and Mason known as Bholaram & Sons. The proprietor used to stand at the entrance, dressed in striped trousers, stiff collar and black jacket, bowing even to children like myself who used to come in to put chocolates etc. on father's account. (As I grew to puberty, I particularly liked the slabs of Nestle chocolates each of which had a photograph of a Hollywood sexpot in the wrapping.) Years later when I first walked into Fortnum and Mason in London, the smell of the shop and the atmosphere was so reminiscent of Bholaram's in Simla. So deliveries from them continued to arrive, along with those from more minor suppliers. But the second line of defence was my mother's sagacity in having hoarded gold sovereigns (she preferred Victoria to Edward VII) over the years. My father included, we only now discovered that whenever there was any cash in the house, she used to convert it into sovereigns, tucked away where nobody was the wiser. My father said this reminded him of the flight of the last Sultan of Turkey to Nice after the First World War. They had no money, but staff in the Royal entourage discovered that the Sultan, always a hoarder, had large numbers of gold coins sewn into his clothes, and this kept the Royal party going for some time. It was at this time that I also learnt of an incident when I was about three to four years old. In the hot, dry Punjab summer – we were not in Simla that year – I caught an eye infection which for reasons nobody could fathom meant that I couldn't or wouldn't open my eyes. Whatever medical attention was available locally had failed, and on the third day it was a worrying matter. With a weeping grandmother and mother, doleful servants, my father said 'Give the boy to me'. He put me on his lap, fished in his pocket and dropped a gold sovereign on the floor. Apparently, at that enticing sound, I immediately opened my eyes.

We were not entirely without some help. Grindlays Bank (in those days the Coutts Bank equivalent in India) gave my father overdraft facilities without any security whatsoever. Apart from Bholaram's, other essential suppliers provided credit, without even presenting an account unless asked for. The servants didn't press for their wages – this particularly concerned us, because although they lived free, their families in their villages depended on monthly remittances. On a more personal note, my father told me that he couldn't now afford to give me the allowance, earlier visualised, to supplement my Army pay. He tried to persuade me to go to Oxford, and that he would try to arrange a scholarship; but I was too proud to go there as a scholarship undergraduate knowing that I would not be able to keep up with my own kind and be thereby embarrassed. I have regretted that decision ever since, allowing my pride to stand in my way.

A whole way of life, society's structure and much else was destroyed in the Punjab, never to return. Hindus, Muslims and Sikhs had lived amicably side by side for generations, in the villages and in the towns and cities. They celebrated each other's religious festivals, shared in each other's joy and grief, and the religious divide never divided them as finally as the 1947 political divide. However, the Punjab hardihood and spirit meant that in a short time afterwards there was no refugee problem in the North, whereas in Bengal, also partitioned, it continued for a decade or more. Punjabi inventiveness and capacity for hard work did not make them inclined to accept government handouts and sit back bemoaning their fate. The ethos of Delhi and other places changed with the influx of refugees who were showing evidence of their entrepreneurial skills. About the only thing the Punjabi will not do is to go into domestic service. I hardly knew of anyone with Punjabi servants. As in many cases, other households' outdoor staff would consist of Poorbis from Orissa who made excellent gardeners, while people from the hills and in some cases, Pathans, were the usual order for indoor servants.

I would have need of all these hardy qualities and characteristics as I left home to join the Indian Military Academy in Dehra Dun and eventually my regiment, the 2nd Royal Lancers (Gardener's Horse); although in retrospect I don't think I was well equipped enough to adapt, and accept the catastrophic changes that had taken place in the beloved country and province of my birth.

5
Indian Military Academy

The contrast between the comparatively sheltered and leisured life I had led at home and Aitchison, and what was to follow at the Indian Military Academy could not have been greater. The colours of our IMA tie – red and grey known as Blood and Steel - are an apt indication. In the First Class military compartment of the night train to the Academy, there were a few faces that I recognised from Lahore, but none from Aitchison; my contemporaries from there returning to their States, estates, with two or three going on to Oxford or Cambridge. The truth was that from my generation I was probably the only one who had to earn a living, the rest following in the footsteps of their forebears needed do nothing except play cricket or polo for the rest of their lives. Of the five of us in the compartment, two were destined to reach the rank of Lt General, one to commit suicide some years later, one eventually to die of a heart attack while indulging in an energetic bout of love making, and myself with an uncertain future vaguely predicted in my horoscope cast at birth by the family pandit (priest). Our documents described us as 'Gentlemen Cadets'. To get to this stage – described in the British and Indian armies as the lowest form of existence – I had had to pass a Regular Army Selection Board with physical and mental tests conducted over three days in Meerut, the place where the Indian Mutiny began in 1857. The tests were designed, and very scientifically so, to test our qualities of leadership. At the end of the tests, Col. Black as the Head of the Board gave us a kindly pep talk. 'Gentlemen, those of you who might be disappointed by not being selected should not be downhearted. You will probably be successful in other fields. All we have to do is to assess whether you have the qualities required of a Regular Officer of the Indian Army'. I was overjoyed to have been selected, though I'd never had a moment's doubt that it would be so.

There was little sleep that night on the train. With the arrogance and confidence of youth, we reminded each other of what splendid chaps we were, budding Alexanders, Napoleons or Wellingtons, looking forward to the red carpet awaiting us at Dehra Dun, our destination. Not only was the red carpet missing when the train pulled in around dawn, but we were rudely brought down to earth. As we were collecting our luggage on the platform, a stentorian voice boomed out, 'All here for the IMA go to the truck outside; get a move on and if you can't find a coolie for your luggage, carry it yourself, Gentlemen Cadets, sir'. This was our introduction to our NCO instructors, British and Indian, to become only too familiar shortly. The truck was a three tonner, surely the most uncomfortable vehicle in the Army, or anywhere. We jolted along the four or five miles to the IMA, where we were told of the companies, and corresponding accommodation, to which we had been posted. My company quarters were about a quarter of a mile away from where the truck dropped us, and the effect of conveying the luggage there, plus our reception at the railway station, jolted me into the realisation of how different life was going to be.

The Indian Military Academy was founded in the early 1930s to train regular officers for the Indian Army. Until then, Indians along with their British counterparts had gone to Sandhurst. Its main buildings and its hallowed Drill Square are designed exactly as at Sandhurst. The main Academy building, with the offices of the Commandant and other instructors, its classrooms, library, imposing corridors encompass the Academy Hall, known as Chetwode Hall after the C-in-C of the Indian Army at the time.

(Field Marshal Lord Chetwode's daughter Penelope married John Betjeman, much to her parents' displeasure. When they reluctantly accepted the engagement, Betjeman ventured to enquire of his future father-in-law, 'What now, sir, shall I call you?'. The reply was 'Field Marshal'.) Its walls were hung with various old and laid up regimental colours, and on one side of the considerable length there was a tiered platform from which visiting VIPs and Academy staff looked at and addressed the assembled Gentlemen Cadets. Prominently displayed above this platform were the following words etched in gold – the motto of the Academy.

'The honour and safety of your country comes first
– always and every time.
The safety, comfort and welfare of the men you command comes next.
Your own safety and comfort come last – always and every time'.

I can honestly say that most of us tried hard to live up to this precept.

The front of the building faced the Drill Square, which was considered sacred. Nobody could walk across it. On the other side were two comfortable residential blocks, called Collins and Kingsley after earlier Commandants. They had modern plumbing and most creature comforts, and were occupied by the two companies which had done best in the previous term – champions and runners up. There was therefore a rotation in the occupants each term, but sadly my own company never got there. We were accommodated in wartime built long barracks, with adjoining latrine blocks with no plumbing, and shower blocks, which only had cold water. The temperatures in Dehra Dun waver between freezing and 50°F between mid-November and the end of January, and at least one shower a day was compulsory. The latrines offered the old 'thunder box' facilities, keeping the poor sweepers hard at it keeping them clean. I remember one of them saying to me 'I am happy with the before breakfast sahibs, and the after breakfast sahibs. But the sometime this, sometime that sahibs keep me on my feet all day'.

The entire Academy complex covered several square miles in the beautiful Doon valley which lies between the foothills of the Himalayas and the Siwaliks, a low range of hills much older than the former. It included vast grounds for all the team games, a swimming pool, a nine hole golf course, stables and a Cadets' cinema, where the latest Ealing and Hollywood films would be screened every Wednesday, Saturday and Sunday with no charge for entry. There was a Cadets' cafe supplementing our Dining Hall fare which was good. Each company had its own dining facilities, and the standards of service etc, as in the cafe, would put the majority of London restaurants to shame – but no alcohol was served. The whole area with its well manicured lawns and flower beds has always been beautifully maintained, and the only blot on this sylvan landscape was the dreaded Obstacle Course, which we had to do once a week. There were one or two obstacles which were particularly terrifying, like the nine foot ditch one had to jump; it was filled with muddy water and barbed wire to welcome those who didn't clear it. And there was the Wall. This was a zigzag affair about 40 foot high; one got to the top by climbing a rope ladder, then ran the zigzag on the narrow top of it to a jumping point; directly below this was the first landing surface, 15 feet lower and about three feet square, with another similar contraption another 10 feet down from where one landed back on mother earth. Fear of missing these small landing stages, the sound of the blank ammunition being fired at one to simulate battle experience, a Gurkha section pretending to be the enemy and yelling blood-curdling cries made it all quite an ordeal.

On one side of the Academy lands ran the near dry bed of the Tons river, which was used a great deal for our training in map reading and field craft. On its other bank was the now deserted prisoner of war camp which until very recently had housed German prisoners – we did not put the Italians and Germans in the same camp. It was from this camp that Heinrich Harrer escaped to

Tibet, eventually to become a great friend of the Dalai Lama, and to write the bestseller 'Seven Years in Tibet'. I had the privilege in Frankfurt about 10 years later to meet another camp inmate who escaped at the same time – Rolf Magener. He was by then a Deputy Chairman of the German chemical giant – BASF. I forget the name of the book that he also wrote. Without in any way diminishing Harrer's feat of finding his way from Dehra Dun into Tibet, I feel that Magener's was marginally the greater achievement. He was, probably still is, more English in appearance than German, spoke faultless English, and masquerading as a British Officer, travelled by train to Calcutta which was over 900 miles away. From here he managed to get up to the Indo-Burmese border, and walked over to the Japanese, who took him for a British spy. Lucky not be shot, he finally landed up in the German Embassy in Bangkok to again undergo strenuous questioning. His ordeal finally ended when they got a friend, John Acklin – who later became a director of Hoechst, and also my friend – to fly in from his position as an attaché in the German Embassy in Tokyo, and vouch for Magener. What with war-time checks, not much money, forged papers, the difficulty of getting from Calcutta into the Eastern theatre of war without being accredited to any unit, it remains an amazing feat in the annals of escape.

We were divided into four companies, each called after four Second World War battles in which the Indian Army had taken part, and distinguished itself, viz. Cassino and Sangro against the Germans in Europe, Imphal and Kohima on India's eastern front against the Japs. Each Company had a weekly training programme, each day necessitating several changes of clothes e.g. a physical training period required pristine white shirt and shorts, and if the next period was military history or Greek architecture (the academic side covered a very wide syllabus) to be held in a classroom, we were required to change into drill order – shirt and shorts, stockings and highly polished brown shoes. The period after this may be the dreaded obstacle course, for which we had to change into overalls, ammunition boots, haversack and rifle. About ten minutes were allowed for the change, including the time required to cycle from one location to the other, often nearly a mile away – and then we had to ensure that the cycles were parked in a perfect line, with all the front wheels in alignment, with none even half an inch in front or behind the rest.

To return to the early days after arrival – the hierarchy was soon made clear – all officers were of course called 'sir', as were all Cadets of the senior term, although one didn't salute the latter, only stood to attention when facing or passing them, as also with NCO instructors who were addressed as 'staff', but they always called one 'sir'. At times, the sarcasm and wit behind their comments was marvellous, exemplified by the now legendary shouting suffered by King Hussein of Jordan at Sandhurst from the regimental Sergeant Major while being drilled, 'King Hussein, sir, you are an idle king, sir', to which his Majesty replied 'Yes Staff, sorry'. The first week's training programme consisted mainly with familiarising ourselves with the Academy environs. One training period on the second day called 'Tour of the Academy' gave some of us, myself included, fanciful ideas of a gently conducted tour in a Humber Super Snipe (the favoured staff car in those days) or in Jeeps. Instead, reality entailed being made to run from one place to another for the whole morning – in common with some others I ruined expensive clothing and shoes in that early period before our uniforms were ready – we had been measured by the Academy tailor on arrival.

Our training was divided between the academic and the military. The former was extremely broad based, guided and governed by the precept that one should be able to talk intelligently for three minutes on any subject under the sun, whether one was at a smart dinner party or in the jungle. In one lecture on military history, I was rather impetuous in showing off my knowledge. That particular instructor was not up to the usual high calibre which characterised our instructing staff. On the subject of the conquest of the province of Sind in the 1840s, he referred to General Peccavi being the successful officer in command. I couldn't help jumping up and saying 'No sir, it was General Napier who sent the message "Peccavi" after the battle, meaning "I have sinned", a pun now immortal in military folklore'. After class I was put on a charge under Section 39 of the Manual of Military Law on Conduct prejudicial to good order and military discipline. (This section provides the widest net under which a soldier can be charged, from something trivial like having a twisted boot lace to crimes more serious.) The military training, of course, included obvious subjects like map reading, field craft, weapons, man management and leadership, Army organisation, including the organisations of enemies or foes, past, present and anticipated, and drill. This had to be to Brigade of Guards standard, and we did excel in it. Hours were spent on the drill square practising foot and weapon drill. With over 300 of us on parade, each movement was rehearsed until perfect. 'Gentlemen,' the Adjutant watching the parade would say, 'I heard two sounds; you will do that again'. Those who have not experienced it won't understand the confidence and pride and even exultation of spirit felt by those when hundreds of men act in perfect unison.

All our training was well planned and scientifically envisaged. Our physical fitness was progressively stretched so that eventually we would be able to run five miles, complete the obstacle course and fire five rounds into a target all in one hour wearing ammunition boots, carrying equipment weighing about 14 lbs plus a rifle weighing 9 lbs. There were three training camps lasting a week or so; the first appropriately called Camp Initial was meant to get us used to living in the open, putting up tents and bivouacs etc. The next one, a few weeks later was called Camp Initiative, rather tougher. As the name implied, it was expected to develop and test our individual capacity of initiative, going back to the maxims of our overall training. 'Gentlemen, when you have no orders, and all else has failed – your food and ammunition has run out, there is no support, you and your men are on your own, USE YOUR BLOODY INITIATIVE'. This camp lasted for about a week. We set out in sections of 10 into the wilderness – beautiful though the

Himalayan foot slopes were – each equipped in battle order, one day's supply of sandwiches, and Rs 30 each, (about £2.00 in those days) which was supposed to buy local supplies for the rest of the Camp period. Each morning we received instructions from our Officer Instructor and a map reference about 20 miles away which we had to reach by dusk, where hot rations and some shelter awaited us. On the way we were harried by the 'enemy Gurkha platoon', scaring the daylights out of us in one ambush after another. We scattered, rejoined and regrouped and carried on. Those of us who did arrive at the designated designation were told that due to enemy action, the supply truck had been destroyed, and there was no food. But, if we marched another ten miles into the night towards another destination, we may find another supply base. When we got there, having marched about 30 miles and enduring a lot else, we were informed that the base had run out of supplies, but if by the next evening we made another map reference point, we would find some succour – this was another 20 miles away. This was repeated day after day during the week, while all the time there was deception all around, like pinpointing a particular village as offering friendly shelter, but on arrival to be greeted by a shrieking Gurkha bayonet charge. Even though it was all simulated, I can promise you it was a frightening experience. The initiative element came soon for those of us who discovered it for themselves. Buy food where you could; use local transport – bullock carts hired from the villagers, lifts in the few trucks plying the few roads in the area, using the locals' knowledge of the ground to avoid ambushes and to take short cuts. It was hell while it lasted, but at the end of the week there was exhilaration and increased self-confidence to have come through it.

The last camp before being commissioned was even fiercer. It also lasted a week, and was appropriately called Camp Chindit after the well-known operations in Burma by General Wingate only a couple of years before. It followed the pattern of Camp Initiative, except that the marches were much longer, over more difficult ground – up and down one ridge of mountain to another – heavier equipment to carry, and less villages and transport where one could forage or get a ride for a few miles. The return to the Academy, a hot bath and clean clothes, a normal bed with a manservant waking one in the morning with a cup of tea was sheer heaven, and thinking about it kept me going through the rigours of Chindit week.

There was one valet between four Gentlemen Cadets, and he looked after the rooms and uniforms of all four. Apart from our Mess dress in which we used to dine, all the other items of clothing were sent out to be washed every day; they needed it after the strenuous PT or the obstacle course. I can remember changing as many as seven times a day into the different dress order required at various times. We could be in civilian clothes over the weekends or on holidays, but if we left the Academy grounds to go into the town of Dehra Dun – about five miles away – we had to be in uniform. We were allowed to do this on Saturdays and Sundays, a number of us sharing a taxi, others cycling; we had to back by lights out at 11 p.m. Dehra Dun was a sleepy little town, with none of the sophisticated restaurants and nightclubs that Lahore had provided. There was precious little female company, and of course the few girls from families of friends were not supposed to be messed about with. We soon discovered one or two establishments with a tradition of catering to IMA and officer tastes, and the girls were lively and pretty Anglo-Indians. One of my contemporaries, a rich prince from Nepal, kept an account at one of these places, where some of his friends were also allowed pleasures, debited to his account.

The Passing Out Parade at the IMA is a splendid military spectacle – aficionados of the Trooping the Colour ceremony would not be disappointed. With family and friends in the spectator arena, the thrill of becoming an officer, the anticipation of the junior term on parade that it will be their turn next, the bands and the music (Col Bogey always formed one of the quick marches, as well as the British Grenadiers), marching in slow time up the Academy steps to the strains of Auld Lang Syne, and when the file of the last three cadets has reached the top of the steps, the Adjutant on his grey horse rode up the same steps, and disappeared into the Academy building, signalling the end of the parade. The Cadets being commissioned would by then be putting a single pip on their uniform shoulder straps, officers at last. Some would deliberately seek out any NCO instructor nearby to experience the thrill of being saluted by the individuals who only until that morning had been yelling and shouting at them. That was really a thrilling moment, and we would keep on looking at our shoulders to reassure ourselves that we were officers at last, looking forward to the Ball that night in Chetwode Hall with no PT or obstacle course to worry about the following morning, and the anticipation of joining our respective regiments after ten days leave. The senior officer taking the salute in my term's case was Air Marshal Sir Thomas Elmshurst, Chief of Staff of the Royal Indian Air Force. Before this we had had a number of VIP visitors, including Lord Mountbatten, the Governor General of India. He was most impressive in the talk that he gave us on the qualities of leadership, which were present in abundant measure in his own character. I remember one bit particularly – he was recalling his times in the very recent past as Allied Commander, South East Asia Command. The second Chindit operation was then imminent, with two clearings in the Burmese jungle having been chosen as the dropping zones for our paratroopers. These had been respectively named Leicester Square and Piccadilly Circus. For the purposes of the operation, the latter was preferable, offering the prospect of fewer casualties. At the eleventh hour, it was discovered that the Japs were aware of Piccadilly Circus, and had driven stakes into the ground of the clearing to hinder gliders and to impede the parachutists. There was no choice but to use Leicester Square, where the estimated opposition was going to be far fiercer. In order to keep up morale of those taking part, Mountbatten spoke to the assembled thousands. 'Men, there has been a change of plan; we have decided on a better place. It's called Leicester Square'.

Halfway through our course, each one was asked to list three regiments of choice, in descending order. I filled in the questionnaire as follows, leaving little doubt about my choices.

1.   2nd Royal Lancers (G.H.)
2.   2nd Royal Lancers (G.H.)
3.   2nd Royal Lancers (G.H.)

The regiment had indicated that it would be happy to have me. That had always been the case – you had to be acceptable and accepted so that you did not upset the harmony of the regiment; no point in having a chap who couldn't deal with the 'h' in his speech, and God knows what else. The Colonel of the Regiment at the time, Major General J H Wilkinson, had given his approval. (He was affectionately and popularly known as Silky Wilkie, because he dressed to the point of dandyism, and was reputed to sleep always with a white silk cravat around his neck.) Being rich in his own right he ran a Rolls, for which the Regiment provided its most able and well turned out driver. He had a permanent suite at the Imperial Hotel in Delhi, where he was then posted as Director of Military Training and Director, Armoured Corps; the author Iris Portal who was Rab Butler's sister, had been one of our regimental wives, and she told me that Silky Wilkie was an extremely good ballroom dancer, considered 'too smooth' by his fellow officers. Nevertheless, he was as good on the polo field and in equestrian events as on the dance floor. Before we passed out, we had to face the Appointments Board in Chetwode Hall. This decided or dictated our final choice, and consisted of the senior Academy Officers. I felt reasonably confident as I marched in Drill Order of Dress down the 100 yards or more of the highly polished floor of Chetwode Hall, halted smartly, and saluted the Commandant, flanked by other senior officers, seated on the dais. But, as in all human affairs there is the predictable and unpredictable, the variable in Life. We had heard rumours of a new elite corps being raised – the Brigade of Guards modelled on the Foot Regiments of the Household Division in England; it was the idea of the then Commander in Chief,

Commandant: Saroop, you are top of your term in academics, and near the top in drill and turnout (meaning how smart one is in uniform).

General Cariappa, the first Indian C-in-C, who had only recently taken over from General Sir Roy Boucher. I was soon to hear more than just rumours.

Self: Thank you, sir.

Commandant: Nevertheless, some of your instructors are of the opinion that you should be kept back for another term, because of instances of ill discipline and insolence; but I have decided that you can have your commission.

Self: Thank you, sir.

Commandant: I see you want to go into the Cavalry.

Self: No sir, I want to join the 2nd Royal Lancers.

Commandant: That is another example of your insolence. Have you heard of the Brigade of Guards? It is the Chief's pet idea, and the first officer to be commissioned directly into it will be from your term. I think you will be ideal as one of these, and probably end up shortly as one of the Chief's ADCs.

Self: Silence.

Commandant: Well, what do you say, you young fool? Many others would jump at the chance; it's a great honour.

Self: I am honoured, sir.

To this day I don't know what came over me to agree as I did; it was probably a combination of relief at not being held back, ego boosting at the Academy's staff view of some of my qualities, being flattered at being chosen for an elite corps, but also partly fear about what the consequences might be if I declined. As all this wore off, I groaned aloud – what had I done, I just could not be a foot soldier. There were four of us sent to the Guards, (the other three all ended up as generals) but while our contemporaries went off on ten days leave in their new Regimental uniforms before joining their respective units, the four of us had to report to the Military Secretary's Branch in GHQ, Delhi for an interview with the

Chief dressed in battle dress, because of course the Guards uniform had not yet been designed. In my case, any feeling of self importance at being saluted in the magnificent Lutyens GHQ building was almost wholly eroded by the constant nagging worry about what I should do to get out of the scrape into which I had got myself. After a number of sleepless nights, good old faithful Bhopal Singh drove me to GHQ in my father's brand new Plymouth, probably the newest car in Delhi at that time because there had been no new cars in India during the war, and to obtain one of the latest models needed a Government permit. As I got out I got some curious looks from some senior officers and brass hats who were arriving either on bicycles or in tongas (one horse transport).

We four young officers then went through a chain of meetings on the first day, all very agreeable and civilised, with tea, coffee and biscuits available. We started with a cosy chat with a genial Colonel, followed by an even cosier one with the Military Secretary (technically in overall charge of the postings and records of every officer in the Indian Army), a General Sheodutt Singh, Henry to friends, a Rajput aristocrat, pre-War Sandhurst and the very epitome of a cavalry officer with his elegance and casual air. The general tone of all the meetings was how lucky we were to be the first to be selected for the Guards, including at the final meeting that day with the Adjutant General who though also a cavalryman was uncharacteristically rather cold and formal – 'Chief's Own' is how he flatly described us. The next day we were due to be presented to the Commander-in-Chief.

I had by then made up my mind to redeem my earlier cowardice in front of the Appointments Board, and took a chance. Without any appointment, I knocked on the door of General Wilkinson's Personal Staff officer, a Colonel Puri of 16th Cavalry, to be received with a smile and the remark that my call was not totally unexpected. He was aware of the whole background, and went into the General's office, emerging a few minutes later saying the General would see me straightaway, but he was in a foul mood with me. I marched in, saluted, and not asked to sit down, not even to stand at ease – poor old

Puri had to do the same. Wilkie glanced at me for some time, adjusting his monocle and then for the next few minutes subjected me to a well deserved tirade which made me feel thoroughly ashamed and embarrassed at the fuss I was causing. 'You are a bloody fool, Saroop. Why did you do it? The Regiment was waiting for you, and I've told them that should you ever manage to join them, they are to knock the spots off you. I could talk to the Chief, but he would probably feel I was taking away one of his boys. When you see him tomorrow, it is you who have to tell him that you don't want to go into the Guards. He will probably throw you out into the Supply or Ordnance Corps, but I will fish you out of there. Let me see what you are made of. Now get out, you have wasted a lot of people's time'. Puri kindly gave me a cup of reviving tea in his office, and confirmed there was no other way out. 'Look at it this way', he said, 'your courage and mettle is being tested before you have even been in action'.

That night was the worst of all. Only those who have served in the forces would appreciate the terror a 19-year-old would feel at the prospect of having to confront his C-in-C and tell him what he didn't expect to hear. More than that, the Chief had the reputation of being a most honourable man, a firebrand and stickler for discipline; he would probably regard my action as dishonourable, and I couldn't argue with that. What a first few days of the glories of being a Regular Officer! With the three others, I reported to the C-in-C's suite next day at the appointed time. In the ante room leading to the Chief's office, I barely had time to reflect that earlier occupants had been legendary Field Marshals like Birdwood, Chetwode, and only very recently Wavell and Auchinleck. This room had a full length mirror to inspect oneself, and ensure that there was not a hair out of place. We were reminded again how particular the Chief was on turnout, and after a few minutes marched into his office. With my mind in turmoil I don't recall any detail of it except its enormous size and equally large desk. Standing in the room were the Adjutant General and the Military Secretary. For reasons I can't remember, I was the first in line although not the senior most of the four. The C-in-C rose from his desk – he was a commanding figure full deserving of the affection and respect in which he was held – and came towards me.

'What's your name?'

'Saroop, Sir'.

'What battalion are you going to?'

'Your old regiment, Sir, now being reformed as 4th Guards'.

'Good boy; look forward to seeing more of you.'

Sweat was pouring down my legs, although they weren't shaking. If I didn't say something now, I would never respect myself again. He had passed on to the third in line when I plucked up enough courage to say 'Could I say something, Sir?'

'What?' was the pistol shot response, as he turned towards me.

'I'm very sorry, Sir, but I don't want to go into the Guards at all'.

There was a stunned silence for a few seconds, until the Chief turned to the Military Secretary; 'Henry, what's wrong with the boy?'. The reply was, 'I don't know, Sir, he was all right yesterday afternoon.' The Chief was silent for a few seconds, I expected the worst, and then he uttered words I have never forgotten, characteristic of the courtesy and humanity of the man.

'Henry, I do not want an Officer in the Guards who doesn't want to be there. POST THE BOY TO WHEREVER HE WISHES TO GO'. No question of being thrown into some dull Corps, no need for General Wilkinson to do his fishing act. The rest of the proceedings were a blur, except for the Military Secretary's parting remarks, 'Report to my office tomorrow at 10.00 hours and collect your posting orders to 2nd Royal Lancers (how did he know?), or would you rather collect them from General Wilkinson's office?' (He did know; had the two cavalrymen colluded?) I almost danced out of the GHQ building to Bhopal Singh, who could read the news from my face as all the servants had known my anxiety over the past few days. I told him that before he drove me to

Chaudhri Sahib as my father was known. 'Drive me to Connaught Place where Phelps the regimental tailors are so that I can be measured for the 2nd Royal Lancers uniform'.

Apart from redeeming my self respect, I do not feel proud of this incident and the events preceding it, and I was made aware of it that evening at the dance being held in the Queen Victoria Road Officers' Mess. Word gets around very quickly in the Army, and before the sun finally set on the Empire, there was a saying that if a rumour started at breakfast in the War Office in London it would be in Hong Kong before dinner. Although a number there praised my courage, many turned their backs on me. I deserved it. In 1980, the retired Field Marshal Cariappa was invited to England by Her Majesty's Government, and the programme included luncheon at Buckingham Palace and the Royal Box at Ascot etc.

My wife and I were present at a dinner thrown for him by the Military Adviser at the Indian High Commission. The Field Marshal told me that I was following the traditional path of Army, business and politics. I told him I had never forgotten his kindness. He had forgotten, and I reminded him of the details. A measure of the man was the incident during the Indo-Pakistani war of 1965. He had by then retired, but his only son in the Indian Air Force had been shot down over Pakistan and was a prisoner of war. Field Marshal Ayub Khan was then President of Pakistan, and he sent the following cable to Cariappa. 'Your son safe; staying with me in my house', signed Ayub Khan; to which the reply came, 'Please treat all Indian PoWs equally kindly. They are all my sons'. Signed Cariappa.

Field Marshal Cariappa died a few years ago. His last few years were spent in the Military Hospital in Bangalore, looked after with affection and loyalty. A bugler from the garrison would play Reveille in the garden outside his room every morning, and Last Post every night, with a Piper every evening marching up and down outside playing his favourite airs.

Sir Chottu Ram electioneering on an elephant.

Twentieth Century's first Asian Parliamentary Candidate with past leader.

Cavalry Memorial Sunday, Hyde Park; author centre left.

Royal Ascot 1951 – Churchill with Sir Khizar Tiwana.

On being commissioned into 2nd Royal Lancers (Gardner's Horse).

Sir Sikandar Hyat with Churchill and Field Marshall Lord Wavell, Cairo 1941.

Greenwich 1979 Election Meeting supported by Lord Home.

Sir Sikandar Hyat, Punjab Governor with staff.

The Prime Minister being received at their dinner by author and wife.

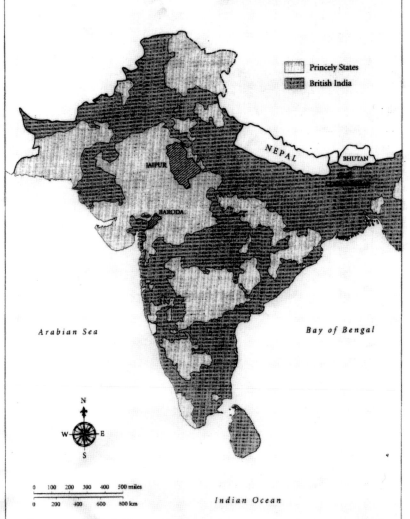

British and Princely India 1858–1947
showing the boundaries of Baroda,
Cooch Behar and Jaipur

Princely States
British India

NEPAL

BHUTAN

JAIPUR

BARODA

Arabian Sea

Bay of Bengal

N
W—E
S

0 100 200 300 400 500 miles

0 200 400 600 800 km

Indian Ocean

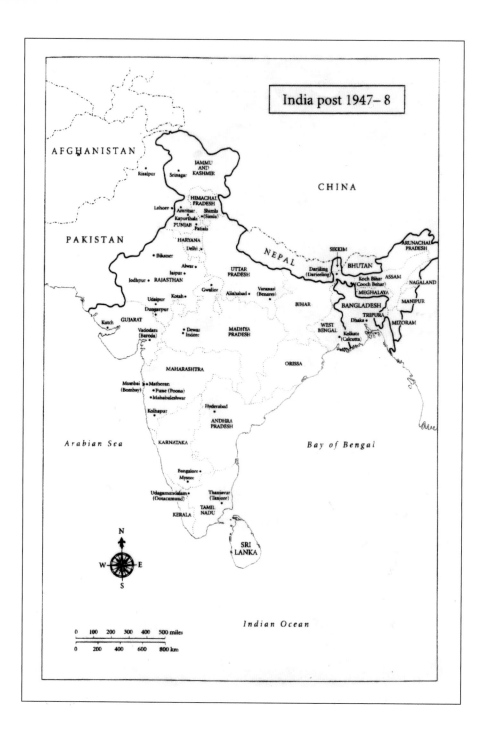

India post 1947–8

6
The Regiment

The British and Indian armies are based on a regimental system, recruited on a regional concept in the British, and a class concept e.g. Jat, Rajput or Sikh in the Indian. A historian once remarked that the British and Indian are not really armies, but a collection of regiments. One joins a regiment, and not the army, and this is particularly so in the case of the cavalry. The system has stood the test of time and battle for at least three centuries.

One of a number of dormant titles is the Barony of Gardner of Uttoxeter. It has three lines of claimants, in the UK, in Australia and in India. Living in modest circumstances in a village between Agra and Lucknow is the senior claimant of the line founded by Lt Col William Linnaeus Gardner, whose elder brother was an Admiral of the Blue under Nelson, later MP for Westminster and the first Baron Gardner of Uttoxeter. With the shameful recent expulsion of the hereditary Peers from the House of Lords, these claims may now be academic but the story of the Gardner family around the world, in the American colonies, in the UK and in India is an epic romance. This is not the place to repeat it, but it is fully covered in my biography of Col Gardner, entitled *A Squire of Hindoostan*.

William Gardner was born on the banks of the Hudson River in Livingstone Manor after a Livingstone daughter had married his father, a King's Officer on whose head the American rebels had put a price. With the help of his Livingstone and De Stuyvesant relations, he escaped back to England, but young William spent his childhood in the American colonies until he and his mother rejoined his father in England. He was born when the British Empire was being lost in the West, but another Empire was burgeoning in the East.

Gardner came to India as a King's Officer, and not as an Officer of the East India Company, in the early 1790s then resigning his commission but staying on in India as a soldier of fortune with different Maharatta princes. In 1809, having returned to the fold, he was asked by Lord Lake to raise a regiment of irregular cavalry which bears his name to this day. During the intervening adventurous years, he married a Princess of Cambay, who was also the adopted daughter of the then Moghul Emperor in Delhi. As part of her dowry, she was given huge tracts of land not far from Agra, and the Gardners lived and entertained there in style until his death in 1833. He never returned to England, and his wife died from grief very shortly after his own death. Theirs was a most romantic love story. Forever retaining the ways of the English gentleman, which he was, he died an Indian squire which he had become.

An additional interesting connection was that the Princess's sister married another English officer named Hearsey, and they also owned vast estates including huge chunks of Dehra Dun where the Indian Military Academy was sited over a hundred years later. Hearsey also raised a regiment called 4th Bengal Irregular Cavalry, and it was entirely in the fitness of things that the two regiments were amalgamated in 1903 to form 2nd Lancers (Gardners Horse). One of the Hearseys, General Sir John nipped the Indian Mutiny in the bud in Barrackpore in 1857.

From its raising in 1809 as Gardner's Corps of Irregular Horse, to the present day as 2nd Lancers (Gardners Horse) the Regiment went through a number of change of titles including 2nd Bengal Lancers, and finally as 2nd Royal Lancers (Gardners Horse) from 1935 until 1950 when India became a republic, and 'Royal' had to be very sadly dropped. Lord Anglesey in his *History of the British Cavalry* describes it as one of the most distinguished cavalry regiments, its battle honours ranging amongst many others from Burma, China, France, Mesopotamia and the Western Desert in the Second World War. It earned a VC at Cambrai (which is now celebrated annually as Cambrai Day) in the First World War, and refused three times to surrender in the Western Desert when Rommel required them to do so, the Regiment then fighting his Panzer tanks equipped itself with only two pounder guns (pea shooters) mounted on trucks. Until the dreary advent of socialist India, it always had Royal and Princely connections. His Highness the Maharaja of Bikaner, famous for his own Camel Corps, was Colonel of the Regiment for many years. His intimate friendship with His Majesty King George V secured its closeness to Royalty, and a Prince Waldemar of Prussia served in it in the last century. A member of the Hearsey family always served in it until the 1930s, and though sadly there was a long gap with no Gardner in its lists, a Lt. Col. Gardner descendant of the founder, commanded Gardner's Horse recently in the 1990s. The first Indian officer to be commissioned into it from Sandhurst shortly after the First World War should have been Iskander Mirza, later destined to be President of Pakistan, but the Regiment said it would only accept a prince; and therefore the role fell to Maharaja Rajendrasingheji – known affectionately as Reggie – a scion of the princely state of Nawanagar and a nephew of the great cricketer, Ranji. Reggie earned a well deserved DSO in the Western Desert when he led his squadron to safety through German positions after the Regiment had spurned Rommel's three offers to accept surrender. Reggie became the first Indian Commandant in 1943, prior to being posted to Washington as the Military Attache at the British Embassy. He achieved undying fame by his answer at their reception, when asked a question by a doughty member of the Daughters of the American Revolution. She was naturally most impressed by his Bengal Lancer uniform and even more so by his wife's exquisite jewellery and sari: 'Colonel', she said, 'how do the lovely Indian women tie their saris'?, to which Reggie replied, 'Madam, I have no idea; I have only untied them all my life'.

It was my privilege to have known him. Whilst still a senior schoolboy, he had permitted me to spend a bit of my Christmas holidays with the regiment, partly to let everyone assess my eventual suitability. They were in Kohat at the time, a military outpost on the famous North West Frontier, with a factory assembling crude rifles for the wild and unruly Pathans only a few miles away, but nothing could be done about it because it was in tribal territory. If the Officers went to the local cinema, they had to be accompanied by a two man armed escort, and that is fresh in my memory as I sat with two of them watching 'Casablanca' – I haven't since stopped humming 'As time goes by'. The Kohat Club was great fun, and on Dance Nights, I looked on with envy at all the chaps in uniform dancing with amongst others the beautiful Mrs Mukherjee, in those days the only Indian lady on the floor, whose husband was then commanding the Royal Air Force station at Kohat, and destined to become the first Indian Commander-in-Chief of the Indian Air Force, and to die later of choking on raw fish during an official visit to Tokyo.

About this time a new officer joined 2nd Royal Lancers, and I was to have the pleasure and privilege of friendship for many years until the late 70's, when he was murdered, the crime remaining unsolved. When he got off the train at the railroad in Kohat, the Regiment had to send extra trucks to accommodate all his luggage. His Rolls with chauffeur arrived the next day. All of us those days in India travelled with huge black tin trunks, long enough to take uniforms or suits without having to fold them; these trunks were marked in white paint with one's name, rank and regiment. In his case the markings on all pieces of his luggage read:

'*2nd Lt Prince Edward Man Singh of Bharatpur*
2nd Royal Lancers'

When a fellow officer in the Mess diffidently enquired about the 'Edward', the lofty reply was 'The Duke of Windsor is my godfather'. Manu, as he was affectionately known, would not follow the accepted war time custom that officers would not use their private transport to arrive on parade. In Kohat, the regimental lines were not far from the Officers' Mess, and the Parade Ground even nearer. For the first few days, Manu was, of course, driven there by his chauffeur. The Adjutant, Bill Bissett, remonstrated with him but to no avail. Manu was then asked to report to the Commanding Officer, and Reggie was civilised enough to ask him to sit down.

Reggie: 'Manu, you know the War is still on and we are in a North West Frontier location'?

Manu: 'Yes, Colonel'.

Reggie: 'Well, all the officers including myself walk or cycle to Parade; you should do well to follow our example '.

Manu: 'Colonel, I am the younger brother of a ruling Prince'.

Reggie: 'Stand up, stand to attention. I am also the younger brother of a ruling Prince, and of a State larger than yours with a larger gun salute; and what is more I may not be Edward VIII's godson, but I am the Commanding Officer of the Regiment, and will tell you what to bloody well do'.

Manu: 'Yes sir', and in future obeyed.

After he left the regiment, Manu went back to Bharatpur and served his state well, being democratically elected to the Rajasthan State Assembly time after time for almost three decades. He was implacably opposed to the ruling Congress Party in Delhi, and its corrupt and power hungry politicians.

By the late 1970s or early 1980s when conditions had deteriorated to an abysmal low, he was reported to have driven around his constituency in a World War II armoured car, flying the Union Jack and shouting 'Bring back the British' through his loudspeaker. Very sadly, he was murdered during this election campaign, at the alleged initiative and connivance of the highest powers that be in Delhi. The same rumour also points a finger at the organiser of the deed, and if correct it could have been someone I know well, and who is related to me by marriage. The new India needed people like Manu, but its new rulers after 1947 did not want true patriots.

The Regiment was very much a family affair, with men whose fathers, grandfathers and other forebears had served in it. In one case, there were about 60 members of the same family who had, at various times, worn its uniform. In battle, this is extremely important. To bolster one's courage there is the spectre of shame in your family, village and community if you are branded a coward. Equally so, the officers lead from the front, exercising command not by virtue of rank, but by the affection and respect in which they are held, not asking their men to do anything which they couldn't do themselves. I had the added advantage when I joined in being posted to the Jat squadron where each of the 120 men knew my family and respected it. This, of course, implied even greater responsibility for me for not only did I have to remember the names of all 120 men and their villages and family circumstances, but I was also expected not to put a foot wrong.

This was therefore the ethos when I reported to the Regiment in Ambala, a well known military station 120 miles north west of Delhi. An established ritual was that of Dining In the new officer. We used to have four Dinner Nights and three Supper Nights in the Mess on Mondays, Tuesdays, Thursdays and Fridays as the former, and Wednesday, Saturday and Sunday as the latter. Dinner Night was formal in Mess Dress – an elaborate affair. You assembled in the ante room full of silver and trophies when the trumpeter outside sounded the first Mess call; fifteen minutes later he sounded the second Mess call after which only short drinks e.g. sherry were served. At the appointed time the Mess Daffadar or Sergeant reported dinner was ready to the senior officers dining that evening. We trooped into the dining room in order of seniority, and took our appointed places, the junior most at the bottom of the table facing the senior most at the head. There was no wine at table those days, because wine did not travel well to India; I think we mostly drank whisky, beer or water, but at the end of the meal, decanters of port and Madeira were circulated clockwise around the table, and glasses charged for the two toasts 'His Majesty The King Emperor', followed by 'The Regiment'. On Supper

Nights, we dressed in dinner jackets and went into the dining room as and when we felt like it, with no seniority, and the atmosphere was more informal. On Dinner Nights, we could only smoke after the loyal toast; Burma cheroots (might have been the odd Jamaican or Cuban cigar), or cigarette, the latter Turkish only; Virginian cigarettes like those which are generally smoked nowadays were considered infra dig, and nobody had heard of Marlboro.

The Dining In procedure of a new officer took place in my first week there, and not until then were you considered to really belong. The junior most officer, myself, is always called 'Mr Vice', not because of any delicious sexual activities, but he is the Vice President of the Mess Committee, with the senior officer being the President of it. At the appropriate moment, the President taps his glass for attention, rises and looks across the long beautiful table with its silver at me, and says, 'Mr Vice, the King Emperor', at which I rise and say 'Gentlemen, the King Emperor'. The decanters circulate, some of us pour Madeira and port into the same glass, and the procedure is repeated for the second toast. On my Dining In night, we trooped back into the ante room after all this, and the signal was given for a bit of boyish horseplay, like jumping over the leather furniture, or hopping onto a senior major's back pretending he was a polo pony – and he had to perform the role. I thought this was all, and great fun too, until the senior officer motioned for order and silence. 'Gentlemen, Saroop's initiation can now begin'. I was told I had to drink a large glass of champagne standing on my head. Now, a glass of champagne is no hardship, but the other requirement was totally beyond me. The penalty for non-compliance was to continue drinking champagne until told to stop, and be properly on parade the next morning at 6.30 am. Only those who have served in a cavalry regiment would recognise the camaraderie; I was carried off to bed, had about 3-4 hours sleep, dressed by my servant and covered for by my fellow officers for any erratic behaviour on parade the following morning. The men knew it all; they had seen it before and enjoyed it. In a good regiment, the men are rather protective of their officers, in battle and in peace. A good example of this was a few years later when I was acting Squadron Leader with the regiment on manoeuvres in the Punjab plains in March - a lovely time of year in the short Punjab fortnight of Spring. The Hindu festival of Holi – sprinkling of coloured water on friends and relations - fell in the middle of this military exercise. Jat and Rajput troops celebrated this with gusto. Being a holiday, a Burra Khana or a big meal was prepared in the men's kitchens, officers invited to eat with them, a great deal of rum drunk by all, and photographs taken for posterity. The officers are normally in blazers, with the men in smart regimental mufti – plain clothes – but their turbans reflecting the Squadron colours. After several mugs of rum, I sat down to lunch with my squadron, a delicious meal. What I did not know what that the first course 'pakoras' – nowadays known throughout the British Isles as 'bhajis' – were spiked with an item called 'bhang', a mild form of opium, taken now and then by most of the farming community in the Punjab. I remember well the jollity of that lunch, but nothing afterwards. I woke in my tent about twenty hours later, and discovered that I had completely passed out, my men had carried me back to be put to bed on my camp cot, and any enquiries from the regimental HQ about a mile away about my whereabouts were answered with 'Sahib has gone on a reconnaissance in his Jeep'. What loyalty, and I had the best long sleep in my life!

Peacetime soldiering has always been boring, but it was particularly so for the Indian Army when I served in the late '40s and early 50s. For the last 150 years, there had always been the prospect of action somewhere, overseas and if not on the North West Frontier. Now, with Nehru's mistaken foreign policy of non alignment, and equally juvenile fantasy of creating a third world axis by sucking up to dictators like Tito and Sukharno (Indonesia), there appeared to be no chance of a break from routine. The Indian Army should have been with the British Commonwealth forces in Korea; instead India sent an ambulance unit. Officers like myself tried to create our own diversions, away from the round of Club dances and tennis etc. One of mine was in the squash courts. The day after a big dance, I received a telephone call from a lady I had danced with; she enquired whether I played squash. Nobody else I know has ever enjoyed squash courts as a tryst for an illicit liaison, made all the more delicious because we both courted the danger of scandal, and in my case of a court martial.

Kausali is a small hill station about 5000 feet high, and situated about 63 miles from Ambala; there is, however, a footpath of 9 miles descending steeply to the plains from where Ambala is only 40 miles. One Saturday when there was a Gala dance at the Kausali Club, (not far from a house which Lord Kitchener had used as a staging post to Simla), wishing to go by car as I had been denied leave for the weekend, I made a friend give me a lift. I stayed up until around 4 am, and then in my dinner jacket and with a lot of whisky inside me I started out on the footpath. As the Alpine scenery disappeared and the whisky wore off, I remembered that panthers were rumoured to be in the area. Making as much noise as possible, including singing, which I hoped would keep the beasts away, I managed to get down to Kalka, the town on the plains, and hired a taxi; I got back to the Mess, changed into blazer and flannels, and feeling like death with the day's newspapers in front of me, and demolishing mulligatawny soup, (which we always had on the breakfast menu on Thursdays and Sundays; Thursdays because Wednesday would be a half holiday thereby increasing the chances for officers' inebriation) when one fellow officer came in and said 'Hello, where were you last night'? 'Stalking panthers, male and female', was my reply.

Detail has always bored me – I could never have been an accountant or engineer – and the esoteric mysteries of our tank and armoured car engines always eluded me; although I liked gunnery and wireless, the other two skills in the mechanised cavalry. However, I loved military strategy, tactics and manoeuvres when one fantasised about being in battle.

There is an Annual Confidential Report written on regular officers, and I came to respect the qualities of judgement of ability and character which my seniors possessed. One of my reports read, more or less, 'This young officer is not interested in tactical detail; he looks at military exercises not from the level of his rank, but from that of Wellington; feels he can command armies better than he can command his squadron; his best is excellent, his second best, when he is not interested, is not good enough'. Perhaps one of my reports, could well have read, as in the case of Lord Brabourne telling me about his own Report 'This officer would make a very good civilian'. One of the military exercises I fondly remember entailed my squadron performing duty detached from the Regiment. It was exhilarating, under 20 years old to have my own independent command. We were attached to 7 Indian Infantry Brigade in a support role, but my squadron returned each night to our own 'harbour' or base. After a bath in my tent, I would dress in either Mess kit or a dinner jacket, depending on the day of the week, the squadron trumpeter would stand outside my tent and blow the two respective Mess Calls, and I would troop into the Mess tent with some of our silver on the table. Only those who know will appreciate the joy of feeling clean after a hard day in the wilderness and then dining solitary in a dinner jacket. Could this have been the last time when anyone on his own changed for dinner in the jungle? The Brigade Commander was a Brigadier Kaul, justifiably not held in great respect or affection. Years later as Army Commander he was partly responsible for the debacle and humiliation experienced by the Indian Army when China invaded north east India in 1962. Contrary to all intelligence reports, Nehru refused to believe that his Chinese pals intended to invade, a view in which he was encouraged by the highly controversial Defence Minister, Krishna Menon. I kept out of the Brigadier's way knowing he did not much like cavalry officers. However, among the top brass of observers was the charming Lt. General HH The Maharaja of Patiala and his brother-in-law Col. The Raja of Nalagarh. Little did the three of us realise that within two years time my marriage would make me senior to them in relationship by becoming their uncle-in-law.

Family trees are complicated to explain, but suffice to say that my future wife's uncle was the maternal grandfather of Patiala and the Rani of Nalagarh.

I met my first wife on leave in Simla. Ravi was a beauty with corresponding high spirits – she used to drive her father's Jeep at some speed on twisting mountain roads with only one hand on the steering wheel. Our engagement set two precedents at the time – firstly that it was not arranged by the two happy families, and secondly it was between a Hindu and a Sikh, which she was. Everyone said that my grandfather, if alive, would have been de-lighted, for he was a great proponent of inter community amity. Her father was a great bon viveur, universally known for his gen-erosity, and he gave us a lavish wedding which Simla would remember for some time. He was always affectionate and kind to me, and this continued even after we sadly divorced in 1967. The fault was entirely mine; fates have not blessed me with the ability and capacity to make a good husband.

During a brief attachment to Queen Victoria's Own The Poona Horse, I had decided to resign. The long Army career to which I had looked forward was sadly not to be, because really with the chang-ing social conditions I was finding myself to be a square peg in a round hole. I have been back to both my Regiments several times for the most enjoyable reunions. They and indeed the Indian Army is, if anything, more professional and with greater fighting efficiency than in my days. But the ethos has changed to a certain extent. It is not better nor worse; it is different. A sense of light heartedness has gone, not to take life too seriously, but to look on it as a glance like we did. But I shall be grateful for that short and undistinguished period; the concept of duty and honour, loyalty and integrity, the urge to earn the respect and affection of one's men and for whose spontaneous love and loyalty I shall always be grateful.

The boon of those values forming a layer over whatever few qualities I possess myself were a great help in later life, although I was subsequently to find out that most, if not all of them were not there in abundant supply in business and politics to come.

7

Boredom
of a Boxwallah

'I hear Saroop is going to become a boxwallah', was the comment, accompanied by some hilarity, in the Officers' Mess of Queen Victoria's Own Poona Horse. A boxwallah is a somewhat pejorative term applied to those involved in Commerce and Industry; it literally means the fellow carting around a box selling its wares.

Although I had advised my father that I was resigning my Regular Commission, no suitable employment was on the horizon when I put in my papers; and those days it was not easy to resign. One's resignation had to be forwarded through what was described as 'proper channels' – Commanding Officer to HQ, Brigade to Div, to Corps, to Army, to Command, finally to GHQ where it went from the Military Secretary's Branch to the Adjt-General to the C-in-C, from where it went to the Ministry of Defence for final approval by the Minister of Defence. They were all hurdles, but the two major ones turned out to be my Divisional Commander, and the Minister, who at the time was Nehru, the Prime Minister also looking after the Defence Portfolio. The General commanding our Division called me for a rather painful interview, giving me a proper 'roasting', at the end of which he added,

'You got one of the few vacancies for a commission which could have gone to somebody else, who is now probably working as a clerk in Grindlay's Bank'.

'That, sir, is precisely why I wish to resign because no potential officer of the Indian Army should be working as a clerk. I do not like the changing social conditions.'

'You are impertinent and insubordinate. Put him under arrest.'

At this moment, my Commanding Officer present at the interview intervened, but not too wisely. He said,

'If I may be allowed to say, General, that could be slightly embarrassing. The boy's family has influence.'

A red rag to a bull. 'March him out, give him the toughest duties while he is still here, and I would be bloody glad to get rid of him', were the General's last words.

My application made its upward progress through the proper channels, and at Western Command H.Q., there was the benevolent presence of Gen. K.S. Thimmaya, known as Timmy, who via Sandhurst, the Highland Light Infantry, and a distinguished war career was G.O.C. in C Western Command. A few years later, he was the top military officer in U.N. peacekeeping operations in Korea and Cyprus. He kindly saw it through to G.H.Q. and beyond to the Ministry of Defence, the final hurdle to be tackled with some finesse. Nehru had a short temper, and if he were looking at papers to approve or sign when in a bad mood, the odds could be against. Fortunately, it went off like clockwork – the very senior civil servant at the Ministry chose the right moment, with my application in the middle of a sheaf of routine papers requiring Nehru's signature, he being in a good mood signing blindly that day. Actually, I suspect that if he had known the whole background, he would have approved my application with great glee, getting rid of me whose family in his view were collaborators of the British.

However, while progress was being made on my release papers, there was still no suitable employment in prospect. Earlier, when I had put the matter to my father who knew nothing about business, his comment had been that did I wish to become a shopkeeper or a petrol station attendant. He had just about heard of firms like Imperial Tobacco or Imperial Chemical Industries which those days offered a good career pattern. 'I have only one torpedo I can fire', he said, 'and I'll write to my old friend and colleague Sir George Abell.' Sir George had also worked under my grandfather, and was then in a senior position in the Bank of England. His warm reply was neither too encouraging nor discouraging, and it started off by saying that he had not seen me since I was a boy, didn't quite know how I had turned out, and in any case young men like me should be serving India because that's where they were needed (he didn't know that Mr Nehru didn't quite see it that way) and so on. However, he would see if there was anything he could do. And that would have been the end of the matter except that a few weeks later in the pigeon holes for Officers' Mail in the Mess, I found a letter which contained one of the best pieces of good news that I have ever received. It was from the senior Deputy Chairman (of which there were three in India, the Chairman and largest share-holder being the 1st Lord Catto, then still Governor of the Bank of England notwithstanding its recent nationalisation), and it read something as follows:

'Dear Sir
The undersigned has been informed that you are interested in a career in Commerce & Industry. Should this be the case, he would be happy to meet you to discuss the matter if you could arrange to visit Calcutta.
We would, of course, pay all travel and other expenses.
Yours faithfully
Sd. Sir Alexander Sim'

The company in question was Andrew Yule & Co Ltd, and in those days not only perhaps the largest British investment in India, but also perhaps the same in its scale of operations. It was a naturally evolved conglomerate before anyone had thought of the word. It controlled around 79 companies, quoted on the Stock Exchange, covering tea, jute, paper, shipping and port lighterage, engineer-ing and insurance. One of its coal companies owned the largest coal mines in Asia, there were big chunks of real estate in Calcutta equivalent in London terms to bits of Bond and Jermyn Streets, and it had the majority shareholding and controlling interest in the largest circulation English newspaper called The Statesman. Andrew Yule had been founded in the 1890s by two Yule brothers, one of whom was later one of the founders of the Indian Congress Party. Since inception, The Statesman had always taken an independent political line and was not necessarily always pro-government. The man who had really built up the company before the First World War and subsequently was Sir David Yule who died so rich that the value of his probate required special paper to be printed by the Government Printing Press. He died in 1929, and stories of his meanness abounded. During George V's visit to Calcutta in 1911, when Yule was to be invested with a knighthood, he rubbed ink over his frayed black coat rather than buy a new one. When the King Emperor graciously visited one of Yule's jute mills, reputedly the most modern in the world, the mill manager was reprimanded for putting out brand new jute matting at the jetty where the Royal Launch was due to berth. Shortly after the First World War, David Yule brought in a fellow Scotsman, Sir Thomas Catto (eventually Lord Catto of Cairncatto) as a partner, who became the majority shareholder. After Sir David died, Andrew Yule became very much a Catto concern, with links to Morgan Grenfell in London and JP Morgan in New York through Catto's contacts in America where he had worked for H.M. Government during the First World War, and deservedly got his knighthood and eventual peerage. At this time, the Indian subsidiaries of ICI and British American Tobacco were considered very much the new boys, and nowhere near Andrew Yule in size and influence. The latter even after the transfer of power in 1947 was still regarded well in Delhi, partly because of the earlier Yule's role in founding the Indian Congress Party.

I alighted at Howrah, Calcutta's railway terminus, from the air-conditioned comfort of my 24-hour journey, to be greeted by Calcutta's smells, its fetid air and even in January a humidity I had never experienced before. Neither had my civilian bearer and my

101

soldier servant from the Regiment, who were accompanying me. While the other bearer was supervising the collection by coolies of our luggage on the platform, the soldier came up to me and said 'Sahib, what are we doing here? This is no place for us. Please withdraw your resignation and let us return to the Regt.' I kept silent, privately agreeing with him. We took a taxi to the Grand Hotel, and after a well needed bath I dressed in uniform and took a taxi to the offices of Andrew Yule in 8 Clive Row. It was an imposing building, but in a small almost mean street, unlike the imposing locations in Clive Street and Fairlie Place of Inchcapes, Jardines and Gillanders (of which major shareholders were the Gladstones, descendants of the famous Prime Minister). There were a number of immaculately dressed doormen. I was ushered into a comfortable waiting room where I hardly waited at all before being ushered into what was known as the Big Room – a beautifully appointed long room with all three Deputy Chairmen behind their impressive desks, suitably spaced. Behind the centre desk was Sir Alexander Sim. You couldn't help liking him at first sight – stocky, toothbrush moustache, silk shirt and an infectious smile. 'Do sit down, I'll just sign a few letters, and we'll go and have lunch at the Bengal Club.' Soon, we climbed into his chauffeur-driven Rover; (notwithstanding their pre-eminence, Yule's did not believe in Rolls or Bentleys for their directors, rather different from Inchcapes and others).

The Bengal Club was, and still is, an impressive building on the main thoroughfare, Chowringhee. The premises inside would have competed with any London Club, and the membership was restricted to only the top directors of the British companies in Calcutta. I was obviously a bit nervous of how I would perform during what was clearly a civilised interview, but was soon put at ease. Over a gin and tonic, after I had called him 'Sir' a number of times, Sim said, 'No need to say Sir, I am Sandy. We believe in recruiting gentlemen. We can convert gentlemen into businessmen, but it's not easy to do it the other way round. We have no wish to try'. Over lunch the conversation was mainly about golf and polo, and when I stupidly enquired whether Sim would like to see my references, including one from my Commanding Officer, he smiled and said that that would not be necessary. During our conversation at table, a number of his fellow members came over, and each more or less said the same, 'Sandy, it's a few years since we saw a cavalry uniform in the Bengal Club, could you introduce me to your guest?' These were Chairmen of the other commercial giants, Pakes of Inchcape, Sir Alan Eliot Lockhart of Gladstone Lyall, Parish of Gillanders, Foster of ICI and so on. At the end of the meal, Sandy Sim said to me, 'They are all looking for people like you. If you like the cut of their jib better than mine, say so and I'll talk to them. They will ask you to join them, you don't have to apply.' Fortified by his charm and the excellent lunch I replied that I wouldn't dream of it and would be very happy to leave my fate in his hands. Back in his office, Sandy scribbled a few figures on a small piece of paper, which I have still kept. They added up to a salary equivalent to about £700.00 pa, plus free accommodation, servants, car and all domestic utilities. In addition, Yules would pay my entrance fees to two Calcutta Clubs and their monthly subscriptions. In the context of that period, the terms could not have been more generous particularly as they included Home Leave terms, six months every three years to England plus a fortnight's local leave each year in between.

When I think of directors and executives these days who are afraid of being away from their desks for a week in case it disappears in their short absence, it was a testimonial to the stability of the times. Moreover, when your Home Leave ship docked in Southampton or Tilbury, a company car would be yours to use during your leave, to be shipped to India to use during your next tour of duty, to be sold and for you to keep the sale proceeds until your next Home Leave for the process to be repeated. Of course, I was delighted to accept, but asked a stupid question, 'Will I get a written contract, Sandy?' He smiled and said that although that was the general practice with almost every other firm, Yule's believed in a gentleman's word. He had been with them for over 20 years, was due to retire the following year, and he had never had a contract, only a slip of paper like the one he had given me.

He then said that as soon as the Army released me, they would like me to go to England to spend a year divided between Morgan Grenfell and Yule Catto, their English arm in the City. I would be paid 5 guineas a week, but they would make a special additional allowance of three guineas a week because of my previous Army service. This was all welcome news, to be catapulted from being in an Army tent as I then was to the visualised fleshpots of London. My Army papers came through shortly afterwards, and after a number of drunken farewells with the men in my Squadron, and the dining out evenings in the Mess, I eventually embarked in Bombay, just recovered from several hangovers. The ship was MV Batory, of a Polish line which had recently been in the news when several of its crew jumped ship in Hamburg to escape to the West. This explained why every cabin had two stewards, a normal one with the other chap from the Polish NKVD to keep an eye on him. The ship was not in the same luxurious class as the P&O and Lloyd Triestino liners who then plied the UK/India route; my passage allowance as a new boy in Yules did not entitle me to sail on these grand lines, and therefore the rest of the passengers were mainly tea planters and other middle ranking boxwallahs and a few junior and middle-ranking Army officers. The voyage lasted 17 days; by the second day various like minded groups and cliques had formed, and I had naturally gravitated towards the Army crowd, which included former servicemen now working in businesses in India.

It was a jolly voyage, with a number of unattached members of the fair gender on board, and these occasioned the running of daily sweepstakes in my group about which one had bitten the dust the previous night, and odds on the others for that particular day. One particular new friend was a Major Bowden, a fellow cavalryman from the 4th Hussars (Winston Churchill's old regiment) who was returning to his Regiment in the BAOR in Germany after a course at the Indian Staff College in Wellington, S India. He was getting off at

Gibraltar with his car, and driving to Vienna to collect his fiancée who was the former daughter-in-law of the wartime Hungarian President, Admiral Horthy, a Nazi sympathiser. Her late husband had been killed in an air crash in the War, reputed to be the work of the Nazis, who felt that he was not Nazi enough. The Admiral had brought in Hungary on the Axis side. Bowden very kindly asked me to his wedding a few weeks later at St Margaret's Westminster, and they made a handsome couple, their society wedding being splashed in all the newspapers the next day. Along with her, he rejoined his regiment as second in command, due to take over shortly as Commanding Officer. To the dismay of his friends, the couple were again in the news a short while later after a most unfortunate incident occurred. The CO at the time was a German hater, did not like having a second in command who in his eyes had married a Nazi, expressed his views volubly one day in the Mess when Bowden could not restrain himself from striking him. It was a sad ending to two promising careers.

A cable was delivered to my cabin while MV Batory was docking in Southampton. It was from Yule Catto's Company Secretary, W H Randall, informing me that a room had been booked for me at the Great Eastern Hotel in the City, less than a minute's walk from Yule Catto's offices in New Broad Street, and suggesting that I come in the following day at any time. The Boat Train arrived at Waterloo Station, and I don't quite know how but the Cabin Trunk which was part of my luggage was left behind when I got into the taxi, and back we went from the Hotel to collect it. There it was half an hour later exactly where it had been forgotten near the Waterloo cab rank; that was the London and England that was at the time. Next day Mr Randall turned out to be an avuncular and benevolent-looking man, whose character fully supported his appearance. Apart from himself and the Assistant Company Secretary Mr King, there were no other executives. It had five or six departments consisting of no more than two clerks each, all of them courteously addressing me as 'Mr. Saroop'. It was quite amusing to discover that whereas the Yule Catto's letterhead listed Lord Catto, Sir Kenneth Mealing, Sir Henry Richardson and Miss Gladys Yule as directors, the rest of the company consisted of only around nine clerks, plus of course the commissionaire, a former Grenadier called Palmer who was a member of the Corps of Commissionaires. It was good for my morale to be saluted twice a day on entering and leaving, something he otherwise reserved only for the directors. He paid special attention to Miss Yule, spraying the office with something she liked when she came to the office to attend Board meetings. She was the only child of David Yule who had built the business empire in India, and remained a spinster because her father had looked on every suitor as a fortune hunter until he died, after which it was too late to marry anyone but a fortune hunter. It was her yacht, 'Nahlin' which had achieved fame or notoriety in 1936 when it was chartered by King Edward VIII to squire Mrs Simpson around the Mediterranean. My training was to consist of attachments to each department in turn to learn the ropes. The pace of work was gentle and civilised, but there were one or two quirky office practices pointing to its Scottish ownership. Although we got a cup of tea in the afternoons, any mid-morning refreshment was absent. All took it in turns to pop out for a cup of coffee or tea between 10.30 and 11 a.m. but it was not done to say, as I mistakenly did initially, that one was going out to the nearby branch of J Lyons to have a cuppa. One merely said 'I'm popping out', and everyone knew what that meant.

We used to get Luncheon Vouchers worth 2s 6d each for each working day, and these would enable a luncheon repast at Joe Lyons, where a poached egg on toast was 9d, a roll and butter 3d, soup 6d, coffee and tea 6d or 5d respectively, a two-course meal including coffee thereby costing a total of around 2s 3d or approximately 11p in today's money. There were a few other restaurants where we could eat a little more expensively, and where the dear waitresses took you over; woe betide you if you sat at a table served by another. Round the corner was Gow's, happily still going, the local Wiltons, but it was financially out of reach. In subsequent years when I have eaten there the memory is always present of a famished young ex-officer looking longingly at its entrance and windows, and thinking of the oysters etc. inside, while on his way to a snack at Lyons. There was also, in Bishopsgate, one of the Pimm's chain of restaurants which was affordable once a month, where I would tear off nine luncheon vouchers for a lunch of smoked salmon, cottage pie and a glass of beer costing in total under £1.00. There was a very pretty girl there at the cash desk, who would say 'See you next month with your next lot of vouchers.' On one occasion, I had the courage to ask her to dine with me. 'You can't afford it,' was the reply.

Both Sir Kenneth Mealing and Sir Henry Richardson were former 'Burra Sahibs' of Andrew Yule's and had had careers in Calcutta spanning around 30 years and retiring from there as the senior Deputy Chairmen. Sim had said in Calcutta that Mealing was waiting for me, making me fancifully think that there was the great man in New Broad Street with work piling up around him, waiting for young Saroop rather like the US Cavalry, to arrive to give him support. It was a few weeks, however, before he took any notice of my existence. With some trepidation I went to his office, but was immediately made to feel at ease. We had what nowadays would be described as a cosy chat, most of the time being devoted to suggesting to me that I should holiday in Austria, 'the peak of civilisation', in his view. On another morning, I was called into Sir Henry Richardson's office. He had joined in Calcutta after the First World War, and had retired just after the Second, a few years earlier. As with the others he was charm itself; 'Mr Saroop', he said, 'I understand that you have served in the Army before you decided to join us. I am very pleased; but I hope they did not do you any discourtesies when you went to meet Sandy Sim, particularly if you were in uniform. You see, I went for my interview with Yules still dressed in my Rajput Regimental uniform, it was 1920 I think, sent in my card, and was ushered in immediately. I wouldn't like it if you'd been kept waiting; it is an insult to one's uniform.' My 'cosy chat' with Sir Henry lasted over an hour, and it would not have been normal not to bask in the glow afterwards of how well I appeared to be getting on with the Yule Catto directors. However, that was also the day of the Annual Calcutta Dinner in the Conaught Rooms, off Holborn. This as always a grand affair, black tie and decorations etc., with numerous tables taken by each of the big British companies operating in Calcutta. Their names sound like a Roll of Honour, and each had an interesting history and sphere of operations. In no particular order, there was Balmer Lawrie & Co, Bird & Co, Gillanders, Arbuthnot, Jardine Matheson, McNeil and Barry, Mackinnon Mackenzie, Shaw Wallace, Gladstone Lyall to name a few of the older traditional ones, and newcomers like Reckitt & Colman, ICI, Tube Investments etc. Some companies like ours had more than one table because of larger numbers. Before we sat down to dine, somebody came up to me and said Sir Henry Richardson wished to meet the new boy. 'But I met him this morning; we had a long chat together,' I said. 'Well, he doesn't remember that, feels he's never met you; just shows what a deep impression you must have made on him,' was the comment. The chief guest at that dinner was Sir Frederick Burrows, who I think was the last British Governor of Bengal. A long-serving railway man, luminary of the National Union of Railwaymen, jovial and stocky, he had been appointed to the post in 1946 by Attlee, with probably tongue in cheek. The very opposite of the usual aristocratic and lofty governors, he made a witty speech that evening, reminding the assembled diners of his very first remark to the Calcutta press on taking up his appointment. 'I am not a huntin' and shootin' man, but I am a hootin' and shuntin' man.'

In the City, like everyone else I wore the uniform of the day – bowler hat and furled umbrella, the nearer it was in appearance of thickness to a rapier, the smarter it was considered. It was no joke to say that most of us would almost prefer to get wet rather than open our umbrellas and have to fold them again. This was quite a task, requiring patience and perseverance, into which I was tutored by the former Grenadier, Palmer, who also did a great job brushing my bowler from time to time. It can honestly be said that at that time mine must have been the only brown face in the City, not that one was made to feel untoward in any way; quite the opposite when girls gave you a longer look, and some old India hands gave you a smile. It would be safe to speculate that at the time there could have been hardly anybody in the City whose family did not have an Indian connection. Some were too young to know. On one occasion, an East End brat walking with his mother, pointed at me and said, 'Mum, is that what Dad calls a wog?' Political correctness was, happily, not then invented.

The City was still a collection of several big holes in the ground, and it was not unusual to occasionally get a whiff of acrid smells caused by the Blitz. There were frequent opportunities for exploration, since a number of times each week I would be asked to take important letters to Lord Catto, either in Morgan Grenfell premises or those of the Bank of England, with Mr Randall repeating solemnly the same instructions each time, 'No Mr Saroop, you will ensure that it is handed over personally into the hands of his Lordship's private secretary, and nobody else'. One of the consequences of this was that I became well known to the imposing pink coated Bank of England commissionaires; we were soon on 'Bert' and 'Sid' terms. They would cheerily wave me in, I became familiar with the corridor and room layout and could find my way around by myself. After this easygoing relationship had been established, I was asked to lunch at the Bank by Sir George Abell, and not being quite sure where his room was, waited patiently for guidance from one of the doormen, who as usual were taking no notice of me until one of them said 'Come off it, you know your way round here, what are you waiting for?' When told that day I wasn't delivering a letter, but lunching instead in the premises, the change in demeanour to formal was instantaneous and worth experiencing. 'Sir George, sir, of course sir, my colleague will take you, sir', and so on. On the way out there was again a farewell consisting of several 'sirs', but the next day we were back to the relaxed 'Bert' and 'Sid' exchanges.

It was some weeks after I joined Yule Catto that I received the summons to meet Lord Catto. I was invited to tea with him at

Morgan Grenfell premises round the corner. Experiencing some
nervousness, and having spent quite a lot of time earlier swotting
up details about A.Y., e.g. what was the total number of companies it controlled, how many of these were tea or jute, and so on,
I was shown into the great presence. This was the only meeting
with him, so all I can remember is an old man, could have been
frail looking – I think he died just one or two years later – but firm
of voice. He asked me to sit down and very shortly a flunkey in
white gloves brought tea in on a large silver salver. My nervousness was unnecessary since I was asked no questions, but just
had to listen to what His Lordship reassuringly had to say, 'I am
happy to meet you, Mr Saroop, and that boys from families like
yours have joined us. Please don't judge the size of our business
with what you see in London, but wait until you get to Calcutta.
You need not worry; you will not have to sell anything, you will
just administer and control others who'll be doing it for you.' This
last bit was indeed welcome news for I've always had a horror of
having to sell, and regard it as below one's dignity. Fortunately,
I've never been obliged to sell anything in my chequered business
career. Sometime during tea, the door opened without anyone
knocking, and I was introduced to Lord Bicester, the other powerful figure at the time in Morgan Grenfells. At the time, they only
employed male staff, including secretaries. It was rumoured that
around 12.30 every working day, Lord Bicester's long-suffering
timid secretary called Jones would help His Lordship into his
jacket, and Lord B would say 'Right, Jones, I'm off to have lunch;
you may now have your dinner'. 'Very well, my Lord.' It was a
daily ritual.

Some years later, his elder son and heir, the Hon John Smith
was my neighbour in Calcutta, spending a year learning about
Andrew Yule's. One Sunday evening his house servant rushed in
to say that he was very ill. I went to him, found he was running a
very high temperature, and got him into Middleton Nursing Home.
By Wednesday morning the poor chap was dead of meningitis
which he appeared to have contracted in the pool of the Calcutta

Swimming Club on Sunday morning. We were all shaken and saddened at this sudden death of a young, jovial and very likeable young man, but nobody more so than David Macmillan, who was the No 1 of A. Y. at the time. It was he who had suggested to Lord Bicester that young John should do a short stint with us in Calcutta on his way to Australia, and he held himself responsible.

I had taken a flat in Clarges Street, Mayfair in what used to be described as 'gentlemen's chambers'. I had a sitting room, a bedroom, and bathroom on the first floor of No 13, with a small balcony. There was a resident manservant called Tom who looked after my wardrobe etc, and brought me tea and toast every morning, but there was no breakfast provided. All this cost me 7 guineas a week, leaving me with the remaining guinea to pay for my monthly pass on the Underground from Green Park to Liverpool Street. So, in Micawberish accounting, I had a roof over my head, uncooked breakfast, luncheon vouchers, but absolutely nothing left over for anything else including dinner. It would have been a dire situation except for an account which my father had had for years with Grindlays Bank in Parliament Street, and which he permitted me to use for modest withdrawals, and I kept his trust.

Not very far in Down Street lived Sir Henry Craik, KCSG, KCIE etc. who had been Governor of the Punjab when my grandfather was a Minister, and who very kindly invited me to a drink one evening, to be followed by dinner at the nearby Cavalry Club. Craikie, as he was popularly known, had lost none of the elegance which I had admired as a boy in Lahore and Simla. Always fastidiously dressed, he sported a monocle, and a grey Homburg hat. Although no longer ensconced in the splendours of the Governor's residences in the Punjab, he lived extremely well, with a manservant in attendance, serving us our pre-dinner drinks. We then adjourned to the Cavalry Club in Piccadilly, my first visit to premises that have given me so much pleasure over the years, and became my first London Club. With characteristic English quirkiness, in the Cavalry Club one lunches and dines in the Coffee Room, where coffee is not served and you move to the Smoking Room for that purpose. Our Coffee Room has marvellous views of Green Park, and when we had ordered, Sir Henry said he did not wish to ruin my appetite, but did I know what those mounds were in the Park? He then informed me that those raised protuberances were mass graves of the people who had died in the City during the great Plague, and their bodies had been brought for burial in what was then open country to the West. Over dinner, Sir Henry also said that I should have a London Club, and I was happy to say that I had just been proposed and seconded for the Cavalry Club. 'Oh, well, then it's all very simple', said my host, 'I am on the Committee here, and I shall have it dealt with.' I expressed my gratitude, and then ventured to enquire how he was a member, let alone on the Committee as he had a distinguished civil service career but had never been a cavalry officer. He chuckled, and said, 'My boy, as Governor I was also Hon. Col. of the Punjab Light Horse (an auxiliary unit). After I retired, somebody found this out, I was elected a member and shortly after that to the Committee because they said I had time on my hands.'

The Cavalry Club those days was an extremely friendly and jolly place. With all the timidity of a new member, I used to run the gauntlet of being eyed up and down by severe looking senior members, some with very military moustaches, others with just one arm or a leg, or just one eye, and I heard those who had fought in the Boer War reminiscing about Mafeking and Skionkop. But I soon learnt that they were not glaring at me, they were just curious about the new face. They were also extremely tolerant about the hearty and noisy behaviour of us younger members. One who was not quite so tolerant was Field Marshal the First Lord Birdwood, formerly Commander-in-Chief of the Indian Army, whose second daughter-in-law years later was the notorious National Front supporter, and our paths crossed politically. One particular chum of about my age was Peter Martel, son of a distinguished General who had been involved in the invention of the tank in the First World War. Peter and two or three others were particularly boisterous one early evening in the Smoking Room, where Lord Birdwood was reading the evening paper. They paid no attention, got more boisterous, the Field Marshal left in a huff muttering about having a word with the Chairman of the Club. The young bucks did not take to this kindly, and hatched a plot. After a good dinner, they went to Shepherd's Market, and selected the fattest blowsiest tart they could find, enquired whether she would go to bed with a Field Marshal for three guineas. The deal was done after she said, 'Young gentlemen, you should know that for three guineas I would go to bed with a camel.' Somehow they managed to sneak her past the Night Porter, took her to the third floor, gingerly opened the Field Marshall's bedroom door, shoved her inside and fled in different directions. There was hell to pay the next morning. The Committee met, Lord Birdwood fulminated until the youngest Committee member said, 'But, Field Marshal, you must be aware of Club Rules which strictly forbid lady guests in Members' bedrooms.'

The Club had a fairly large membership of those who can be fairly described as characters. There was one who always said the same thing to the waiter in the Smoking Room when ordering his drink, 'Tell the Porter if my wife calls I'm not here.' There was the late Lord Dunsany with a luxurious growth of hair protruding from his ears, and each time the Club barber tried to trim them, he would be stopped with the remark, 'Leave them alone; they keep out the Irish mosquitoes'. Another loveable character was Col. A.D. Wintle of the Royal Dragoons, who had achieved fame about that time for debagging his family solicitor and shoving him out into a Brighton street. Apparently, this gentleman had been dipping his hand for years into Wintle's maiden aunt's estate, and would be a tricky man to sue. Wintle's wheeze was to embarrass him in public, and be thereby sued by the solicitor. The latter fell for it, Wintle was found guilty at the first hearing, won the appeal, lost again and so until the last round in the House of Lords which he won, having conducted his own defence through all the legal stages. Not only was the solicitor's reputation in shreds, but after the House of Lords ruling he was tried for embezzlement and convicted. Wintle always wore a monocle, which he would throw in the air and catch it on the way down in the eye for which it was intended. He was bald, with a depression at the top of his skull; he could balance a glass of whisky or whatever on his head, and dance the fox-trot or the waltz, but not the more energetic rumba or samba.

Poor Sir Henry Craik was once involved in a rather embarrassing incident. He had lost his umbrella somewhere, and those days it was not unusual for the police to apprehend the fellow who had done it. It was bad enough for a grand personage like a Former Governor of the Punjab to have to attend a petty magistrate's court, but it was all made worse when it transpired that the umbrella he was claiming was not really his.

Those days, a three-course dinner in the Club was 7/6d and a four-course with a savoury at the end of it 9/6d – ie around 38p and 47p respectively in today's currency. A pot of tea with lashings of toast served in a muffin dish would cost 6p. The staff were absolutely marvellous, long-serving and loyal. When the new Hilton Hotel in Park Lane was trying to poach our senior Hall Porter, their very generous offer was declined with the comment, 'Here I serve aristocrats and gentlemen; at the Hilton it would only be people with money.'

The first Sunday in May is observed as Cavalry Sunday when the Cavalry Old Comrades march in regimental groups past the Cavalry Memorial in Hyde Park, a Royal usually takes the salute, followed by a religious service conducted by the Chaplain-General to the Forces. After the parade, a very large number of the officers and ex-officers on parade adjourn to the Cavalry Club, which overflows with all pre-booked regimental lunches, and ladies are permitted in all parts of the premises. For over 25 years, the man supervising the table and catering arrangements was Mr Markie, the Dining Room Steward. A few years ago, after he had retired, after the parade on my way to the Club somebody raised his hat in greeting, and it was dear old Markie. He told me that this was the first time he had actually seen the parade, and how impressive and touching it was, and I expostulated that how could this be, when he had been with the Club for decades. 'But you see, sir,' said Markie, 'I had to be in the Club supervising that everything was ready for you gentlemen and your ladies.'

Until the early 1970s, the Club also employed one, if not two, page boys. Whatever their other duties were, they had almost fixed duties in the mornings and evenings. There used to be a chemist not far away in 100 Piccadilly, and Club members must have provided it with regular business. Each morning a page boy would go there for powders which they made on the premises, and which were supposed to be a cure for hangovers. Each evening he would make the same trip, but this time to purchase rubber products for those members who harboured lustful aspirations for the night to follow.

The period with Yule Catto was a happy interlude, and has provided such pleasant memories. It was a privilege to start my civilian career in such civilised and congenial surroundings. Even the humblest clerk wore a hat, carried a brolly, and it gave him a certain status in his suburban home, where his neighbours not knowing exactly what he did, would say, 'He's something in the City.' Alas! the City has changed out of all recognition, and like most changes certainly not for the better.

I sailed from Liverpool on an Anchor Line boat called SS Cilicia, the voyage pleasant and uneventful except for a salutary lesson in Port Said. During the few hours that the ship berthed there, a few young men going out to work in India for the first time and I decided to have a meal ashore. Having found a suitable restaurant, I advised everyone to memorise the menu prices of the items that they had ordered so that we could spot an inflated bill if one was produced at the end. When it came, it was of course almost twice what it should have been. Everyone looked at me. I took charge and commanded the waiter to bring me the menu. He did as he was told, I scrutinised it only to discover that it was a different menu with prices corresponding to those on the inflated bill. Using a political analogy, I lost some votes that evening, my fellow diners losing faith in my claim to local knowledge, including about India.

After a short spell of leave in Delhi, I reported to Yule's Head Office in 8 Clive Row, Calcutta. The site had been deliberately selected by the canny Sir David Yule, as it was half way between Clive Street, where all the big British were, and Burra Bazaar which was the area with the large Indian businesses. Calcutta had been founded in the 1690s by a Scotsman called Job Channock, and the large British enterprises looked like a roll call of Scottish names. Calcutta's wealth was founded mainly on commodities like tea and jute, and earlier ones like indigo. It was a city of decaying Palladian mansions, had once been the capital of India, and the Viceroy's residence there until 1911 when Delhi became the capital was described by Lord Curzon as a plaster copy of his ancestral home, Kedleston in Yorkshire. Once upon a time it might have been deserving of some of the rave reviews it had received from European visitors describing it as the 'fairest city in the East, the most beautiful in the Empire,' but this had not been the case for many decades. Its fetid climate and new slums having grown in every part of the central and outer areas did not make it the most agreeable place in which to live. Having been used to Delhi, Lahore and Simla and one or two other smaller cities in the Punjab where such slums were virtually unknown, it took me some time to accept that next door, on the other side of the garden in the leafy areas where one was lucky enough to live there could be an adjacent area comprising horrific living conditions. Although there were one or two recently-constructed modern blocks of flats, most of us lived on either the ground or the first floor of a traditional, sometimes mock Palladian house with a fairly large garden. Initially, one was entitled to only one air-conditioned bedroom, then two or three as one progressed up the scale of seniority. After a length of time, you were entitled to a whole house, fully air-conditioned. There was an average of six indoor and outdoor servants per household. The air-conditioning was badly needed, as Calcutta has one of the worst climates in the world, with average temperatures of between 80-

90°F throughout the year and an accompanying humidity average of 90% except for a few weeks of 'cold weather' in December and January. There was no such thing as winter, as it was either hot, hotter or bloody hot. I have always hated the heat, which was one of the reasons for exiling myself from Calcutta and India some years later. If possessed of Kipling-like ability, I could have very feelingly written what he did on the subject, of which a short extract below.

'I could never stand the plains
Think of blazing June and May
Think of those September rains
Yearly till Judgement Day.
I shall never rest in peace
I should sweat and lie awake
Rail me then, on my decease
To the Hills, for old sake's sake.'

Curiously enough, the healthiest time of the year was the 'hot weather' period in May and June, when the humidity was low. After the south-east monsoon broke around mid-June lasting till September, the climate was even more appalling in October when the post-monsoon humidity was at its highest. Notwithstanding this, it was then the friendliest place in the world, with a hectic social and sporting life. There was golf throughout the year, polo in January and February, the Royal Calcutta Turf Club active most of the time, tennis, squash and swimming championships, rugby during appropriate seasons, and indoor exercise provided by adultery whenever opportunity permitted. Yet there was hardly any scandal. It was all discreet, although everyone knew who everyone's extra-marital companions were, and there was acceptance that the climate and everlasting marriage did little to encourage everlasting faithfulness. In all my years there, only one divorce took place in our British Indian set. There were cocktail parties and dinners almost every night, and the dress order was usually dinner jackets for men, who mostly sported a sharkskin or linen lightweight jacket. At the first few of these, I couldn't help noting that while I was one of this immaculate crowd, sweat was literally pouring down my legs, and my shirt and collar remained clammy throughout. Yet, it was a gay whirl.

Calcutta abounded in Clubs, the main social ones being the Bengal Club, the Bengal United Services Club, the Calcutta Club and Saturday Club, known as the Slap, while the sporting ones included the Royal Calcutta Golf Club (the second oldest Golf Club in the world, not the second oldest course), Tollygunge Club, Calcutta Football Club, Swimming Club, Squash Club and the Calcutta Polo Club where we played bicycle polo as well. To put it in unashamedly frank terms, there were the Clubs to which one's circle of friends belonged, but there were many others for the others, into which we wouldn't dream of crossing the threshold. These were rather sectarian like the Armenian Club, the Parsee Club and so on. In fact, there was a large Armenian community in Calcutta, and they have a case in claiming that a few of them were there even before Job Channock in 1693.

The leading night club was the 300 Club, based on the old 400 Club in London. It was managed by a white Russian called Boris Lissanovitch, and financed and supported by the then Maharaja of Cooh Behar who was one of the best looking men of his generation, and who had distinguished himself during the war in Burma serving with the 7th Light Cavalry. It had been his idea to start something in Calcutta on the lines of the 400 in London, and it proved a great success. When weather allowed, dining and dancing were outside in the garden, the food was superb and the music heavenly to dance to and holding in your arms one of the beautiful women who was unattainable added great zing to the atmosphere. Many a tryst was made there, many a gay evening while the trysts were still in bloom, a few evenings when both parties realised that the initial tryst had run its course, and some others when the offer of arranging a tryst was declined.

The manager Boris Lissanovich was an enigmatic character. At times he claimed to be a former officer in the Czar's Navy, others a cavalry officer. Like many White Russians in India at the time, he had fled to places like Shanghai etc. to eventually settle in India. He was most entertaining and ran the Club well. The barman, John, formerly employed at the Ritz in London was the only English barman in Calcutta, and had been 'pinched' by H H The Maharaja of Cooch Behar because he loved John's martinis in the Rivoli Bar. After the Maharaja's death, the 300 Club rather fell apart, and Boris took off for Kathmandu where for some years he took over an old palace, and ran it as the Royal Hotel. He was always in and out of prison for something or the other, but everyone treated him kindly. He must have died by now, but visitors to Kathmandu until the late 1980s or early 1990s would remember his restaurant and bar Yak and Yeti, and also John in command of the bar at the Soaltree Hotel.

If I may be allowed to skip a few years the only time I've tried to smoke pot was in Kathmandu. It was the late 60s, the hippy trail led to Kathmandu, and somewhere or the other I'd read that the hippy Valhalla was a place called The Blue Angel – coincidentally about the same time an establishment with the same name was flourishing in Mayfair, owned by a friend Captain Anthony Sykes, but there was no connection between the two. I was in Kathmandu for a conference, staying with Boris at the Royal Hotel, which was also the refuge for various airline crews, Lufthansa being prominent as I saw one evening when Boris asked me to a drink in his suite. Here I was met by the welcome sight of a number of beauties belonging to the erstwhile master race, and our joint claims to Aryan ancestry assisted in feelings of mutual liking. However, I was foolish to waste about an hour of opportunities, and being determined to see what the Blue Angel was like, asked Boris to get one of his servants to guide me. He was doubtful whether they would let me in in my three-piece suit with a double-breasted waistcoat, but the servant eventually found it in a mean little street off a smelly bazaar. It was a November evening, fairly cold, the entrance had no door but thick jute matting to keep out the cold. There was a wizened old Tibetan with a wispy beard who smiled and let me enter, pointing to a circle of about eight or nine mostly English hippies sitting on the floor in a small smoke-filled room. Naturally greeted with some unspoken suspicion, I was allowed to join them, and a little urchin employed there asked me what I would like to drink. 'Whisky and soda, please,' to be told that only coffee, tea or coca cola were available at the vast cost of one rupee, then about 7p. One of my companions asked me where I had heard of this place, and I replied 'King's Road' knowing I was being tested. 'King's Road where?', enquired my interlocutor, and I had the presence of mind to say 'Gee, man, there is only one King's Road in the whole world.' I was then asked if I smoked, said yes to be then asked what did I smoke? Now, I have never had the faintest idea about this sort of thing, still don't know the difference between opium, heroin, cannabis, cocaine etc. but was again alert enough to reply 'Whatever is available.' The ice had been broken by now, and one of them produced a filthy looking pellet which he crushed in his hand and put into a small pipe. He said it was not very good, he'd acquired it in Afghanistan on the way, and if I paid ten rupees (about 80p) we could smoke it communally, and the money would allow him to clear his hotel bill where he and his girl-friend had been staying for a week. Arrears of about a pound for a week's stay! The mind boggles at the standards of comfort and cleanliness in that particular establishment. However, the pipe was lit, started circulating, and I had puffed at it on two occasions when I felt the whole thing was a bore. Whatever it was had no effect on me at all, and I returned to the more familiar anticipation of Boris's whisky and the company of the frauleins.

Coming back to the Calcutta social scene, there were two large hotels – the Grand and the Great Eastern, which had excellent restaurants combining music, dancing and cabaret. The local equivalent to a combination of the Savoy Grill, the Connaught, the Ritz and Wiltons was a restaurant called Firpo's on the first floor of a building on the main thoroughfare, Chowinghee. Its wide verandah served also as a bar, and you had to book a table there as well as in the restaurant, particularly on Fridays, known as mail day. This went back to the days when all correspondence between the large firms and their London affiliates was despatched on Friday mornings implying that the main working responsibilities were over for that week. Shortly after my arrival, although we commenced using Air Mail, a copy of each letter and document was still despatched by sea mail, just in the event of an air crash. Some tables at Firpo's were permanently booked, both in the bar and in the restaurant for regular customers like the Maharaja of Burdwan and Pat Williamson, owner of the Williamson Major Group of Tea Gardens. The food and service were excellent, and its menu rather amusing with dishes grouped under headings like Herbaceous (or veg), Farinaceous, Crustaceous and so on. Lower down the scale were restaurants like the Park in Park Street which advertised 'Cold Beer and Hot Women' for its Sunday lunches; and of course there was the rather louche Golden Slipper, which gentlemen patronised on their own. It was not a house of ill repute, merely one where there were rather exotic cabarets performed by its female troupe. The other cabaret acts at the two hotels used to have female groups brought over from England during the cold weather season; the fairest of English roses, two of them were quite well born, and daughters respectively of an admiral and a judge. Both were fervently sought after, and made good marriages.

The system for election to any of the leading clubs was based on sound common sense, and it is interesting to note that similar procedures have been adopted in one or two London clubs previously well known for the hazards of somewhat arbitrary and haphazard blackballing. You had to be proposed by the Chairman of your company, seconded by one of its directors, thereby obviating any doubts about your bona fides and suitability. Before your election you and your wife, if married, were invited to a cocktail party to meet the Committee, so that your wife was vetted as well. I can hear the howls of protest these days from feminists and so-called liberated ladies. I was elected to the Calcutta Club and the Royal Calcutta Golf Club. This sensible system was taken a step further at the latter, where you had two courses, A and B. Before a candidate could come up for election, he had was obliged to play six rounds with his proposer or seconder. This showed that they tolerated your presence on the course, as well as that you understood the general and local golf etiquette. You were then asked to meet the Committee, after which you became a 'B' member and had to wait a further two years before being elected an 'A' member. Ladies were allowed to play on the B Course during the week, and over the weekends only if playing with a member. Quite sensibly, they were not allowed into most parts of the Club premises. One disappointing factor about the Club scene was that the Tollygunge and Saturday Club practised a colour bar, which I had not experienced in London previously or since. Some time after I arrived their policies changed, and a few other Indians and myself being considered suitable were invited to join. We declined on the grounds that if we were not eligible enough to join in the first instance, etc. etc. The Clubs suffered as a result, being subsequently obliged to accept what would be called the second eleven. It is to the credit of the government in Delhi and in Bengal that no legislation was considered, let alone enacted to enforce this. The relevant Clubs just accepted changing times. It has been rightly said that colour bar in Clubs was one of the factors that hastened British departure from India. In all fairness, the fault lay on both sides. Until about the Second World War, many Indian women remained in purdah, and it was therefore not quite in the fitness of things if Indians went to Clubs without bringing in their women with them. Most of the Clubs up country in military stations, some of which were no less grand than the Clubs in Calcutta had more or less solved the problem by the mid 1920s, when Indians became eligible for the King's Commission from Sandhurst, and anybody as a Regular Officer irrespective of colour was also eligible for Club membership wherever he was stationed. There was the famous case of the Rawalpindi Club in the city where at the time of writing the Americans are hunting for Osama Bin Laden. A British cavalry regiment stationed there had an Indian (later to become an able general and well-known as a UN administrator) amongst its complement of officers. The usual custom was that on arrival in a new station, all the members of the Officers' Mess joined the local Club en bloc. However, in Rawalpindi the Club Committee were being a bit difficult about including the Indian Officer. The CO of the regiment dealt with the matter in a manner which became a byword for fairness and loyalty to his officers, and firmness in dealing with ingrained prejudice and stupidity. He informed the Committee (composed of the local general and assorted brigadiers and colonels) that if one of his officers could not join the Club, the remainder would not like to join either, and that furthermore none of the Committee could expect to borrow the regiment's horses in various point to point and other equestrian events. The Committee capitulated. I wish I could remember the name of the particular regiment and its CO, who did a great deal for British Indian relations.

I had become a keen golfer, but never managed to get my handicap into single figures, eventually remaining static at 10. The Royal Calcutta Golf Club was one of the venues of the All India Open, and many tournaments to compete for the number of trophies in its possession, but there were two unusual fixtures. The first one, probably unique worldwide was the Monsoon Cup. It had been instituted decades previously with the purpose of keeping the game going through the rainy months. Each leading firm fielded two teams, A and B, of six players each playing medal rounds. You had to play on, whatever the weather conditions. At times in certain games the water cascaded so fast down the gradient that there was no point in using a putter – you had to chip into the hole. Notwithstanding temperatures of around 90°F, the players got so drenched and soaked that it was quite common to ask for a whisky and soda in mid-afternoon at the refreshment huts provided every five holes or so around the course. If a player broke a hundred for his round, he got his name in the newspapers the next day. The tournament was organised and managed by the previous year's winners, it lasted three weeks, and it was my good fortune that Andrew Yules won it the year I joined (I did not play that year) so that we had to run the show the following year. I was detailed to assist David Watkin who was the firm's leading player, and it was marvellous to be away from the office for three weeks, sitting at the 19th marshalling the players to tee off, look and listen to the pelting rain, and receive their score cards when they returned, muddy and soaked. The winning firm hosted a gala dinner at the end of the event, the dress order naturally being dinner jackets.

Until the late 50s, conventions and almost rules about clothes were strict; for example, for the weekend evening performances at any cinema you had to be dressed in a dinner jacket. I well recall one incident where my friend and contemporary, Michael Chapman, thought he could get away with it in a suit, only to be told in the interval by Nic Stenhouse, one of our directors 'Michael, don't you feel you should go home and change?' Chapman did. On another occasion, I was in the jungles of Bihar with my dinner jacket as part of my travelling wardrobe – as it turned out a sensible precaution. Yule's had leased hundreds of square miles of this area to extract bamboo for our paper mill. Our adviser there was a retired Conservator of Forests of French descent called Augier. He was utterly charming, knew his territory well and was full of sound advice like 'Mr Saroop, if you come across any elephants the best thing is to stop your jeep and be still.' He rated the animal as having the highest intelligence, and quoted the example he had seen years earlier of one who had wrapped its trunk around a tree which it was hitting hard with its head in order to commit suicide; 'only intelligent species contemplate and commit suicide.' The herd to which it belonged watched silently until it succeeded and then carried the body away. Augier and I were inspecting a part of the jungle where the bamboo had flowered – if bamboo flowers, it dies and this means there would be no extraction from that part of the jungle until the clumps grew again. That morning we were suddenly showered with something rather unpleasant; I had driven the open jeep straight into where a herd had recently passed and defecated communally. The accumulated droppings were high enough to come up to the jeep engine.

On return to the forest rest house where I was staying – no electricity, running water etc. I had against advice decided to spend the previous night alone. When all the doors and windows were tightly shut, after the cook's departure, to keep out any marauding animals - including bears which were around giving me one of the most frightening nights I have ever spent in complete utter blackness – I found a note awaiting me from Anna Hamilton-Wright, whose husband was a colleague, telling me that they had set up camp some miles away and inviting me to dinner that night, followed by a shoot. Her p.s. added 'Will lend you a gun, but do bring your jeep as we need it, and the dress order is dinner jacket.'

Bob Hamilton-Wright was a great organiser, and this particular camp was another example of his abilities. Many may have seen a television serial based on the theme of 'Staying On' in which he figured prominently. After dressing by the light of a hurricane lamp but without the aid of a mirror, I arrived at the Wright's to find other guests, amongst them the two young Princes of Jaipur, Joey and Pat who had just left Harrow, whisky heir Andrew Stainton who was passing through Calcutta, and a pretty girl out from England for the 'cold weather fishing fleet' season, but I can't remember her name. We dined around the camp fire with Bob regaling us with the number of buffaloes and goats he had arranged to be tied up as bait for the big game. We set off in high spirits, drove and waited from one bait to another, but finally returned to camp in the early hours of the morning with the night's bag – one rabbit for five or six guns. I was never a great shot, but for the others more skilled it must have been a disappointment almost bordering on a fiasco.

The internal organisation and the efficiency of its systems in Andrew Yule's could be a model for a number of equally sized or greater multinationals, as it could also be one for benevolent employers, should any exist these days. The centre of the spider's web was the Head Office in Clive Row. The hierarchy, in descending order consisted of the three Deputy Chairmen (the Chairman being Lord Catto in London) known as Nos 1, 2 and 3. Under them were the directors in charge of departments responsible for managing and running the different production units e.g. all the jute mills came under the control of the Jute Department, all the tea gardens under the Tea Department, and so on. Each director, depending on the size of his department would have between three and four senior executives i.e. those on home leave terms, below whom would be executives on local leave terms with the clerical cadre at the base. Apart from actual production itself all matters of policy were controlled by the relevant department at H.O. e.g. eventual selling price, amount of production, purchase of raw materials, stores and equipment etc. These systems had many tangible benefits, among them the reduction of any possible corruption in units operating hundreds of miles away, the advantage of cheaper purchase prices resulting from bulk buying, and better management provided by the accumulated experience at H.O. The hub here was the Group Company Secretary, assisted by one or two senior executives. The junior-most of these, like myself, always spent most of his first tour of duty in this role, which provided him with practical experience and knowledge of the whole group, as well as a bird's eye view of the whole industry of India because the wide ramifications of Yule's brought it into contact with almost all sections of Indian commercial and industrial activity. In this department sat the cashier with literally hundreds of thousands of rupees in strong boxes which had to be locked up in a vault at the end of the day under my supervision. If anybody required any cash, he had to initiate a cash voucher countersigned by the director of his department, after which it would come to me, and only with my initials would the cashier pay out; three signatures required before payment, and therefore little opportunity for any hand in the till. If one of our jute mills had to pay one of our coal companies for supplies, a transfer voucher would be signed by the two relevant directors for the necessary sum, and on checking all this, my initials would authorise the Accounts Department to do the cross entry debits and credits, thereby obviating bank charges. We not only operated as a bank but issued our own cheque books which were restricted to directors and senior executives only, and there was no Club, establishment or shop in Calcutta which would not take an Andrew Yule cheque. One of my slightly farcical duties was to inspect the numerous doormen, peons, etc. - known in those realistic days as 'menial staff' - each morning before office hours, to see their uniforms were clean and properly worn, but it was a totally different kettle of fish from the inspection I was used to in my regiment. Those used to or obliged to accept the frantic pace in the offices of current times have little idea of how gentle were the pressures of those times, particularly in an environment like 8 Clive Row. For example, when I was working in the paper department, the mill manager telephoned me in great agitation to say their coal stocks were down to two days' requirement, after which the mills would temporarily have to shut down. Our coal companies were supposed to be despatching the stuff. I telephoned Cathcart-Jones in our Coal Department. 'Tony, pull your finger out,' to which he replied, 'Shut up, I'll speak to the chief superintendent at railway HQ because they are not giving us the rakes or waggons.' The much derided old boys' network solved problems like this quickly and with the minimum of fuss. In those days, the system automatically provided the network. Nowadays they have dropped the two words 'old boys' and you see harassed people rushing around saying 'I'm networking' which I would be ashamed to say because this means I don't know many people. Many think this is progress.

The office hours were nine fifteen to four fifteen, although executives arrived around nine and did not usually leave before five. In the cold weather this meant you left in darkness because of the quirky decision by officialdom in Delhi which had imposed Indian Standard Time on a latitude as far east as Calcutta. We worked half days on Saturdays, and for golfers like myself it meant a mad drive to the Royal's course because you couldn't really tee off after 1.30 pm and expect to finish 18 holes. There was 10 days

local leave a year when the firm would pay your fares to anywhere in India, and for those of us on home leave terms the first
tour of duty was three years, and after that every two and a half
years. The firm paid for the passages of yourself, wife and children to the UK and back, and this passage allowance increased
with each leave, six months each time, although after some years,
you could convert it into six weeks back in the UK every year.
Because recruitment and promotion planning were so regulated,
after three tours of duty almost all the senior executives became
directors in charge of departments, with a fortunate one amongst
them moving up as Deputy Chairman No 3 once every three years,
with subsequent leaps to No 2 and No 1 from which position the
incumbent retired after three years in command, usually with a
knighthood, such being the importance accorded to Andrew
Yules. Because of Calcutta's climate, it was considered the age of
52 was not too young for the directors to retire. The company
gratuity usually ensured enough capital to enable one to buy a
decent property in the Home Counties, and Yule Agency Super-
annuation Fund provided a pension of around £1,000 per an-
num, which in the 1950s and early 1960s could not be considered
ungenerous. There were corresponding schemes on scales appropriate to their position in the hierarchy for every grade of em-
ployee, from the mill and tea garden managers and assistants
known as up country Europeans down to the humblest peon. Yule
Catto and Morgan Grenfell usually tried to find directorships in
the City for the retiring senior executives who were, after all, only
52 years old. Most of us, mainly British but also three or four Indians like myself recruited on these terms were all ex-public school-
boys, but Yules did not go as far as the Inchcape group, who did
prefer to take on honourables, baronets and younger sons. As an
example of Yules' civilised atmosphere, before Xmas each year,
our No 1 would have a cosy chat with each director and senior
executive in the private board room, with a decanter of sherry
and glasses on a side table. Notwithstanding the apparent infor-
mality, one was nevertheless somewhat apprehensive because this

was the annual interview, when over the comforting glass of sherry one was told how you had performed during the year, what your annual increment was going to be, and what was roughly expected of you in the following year. However, during my second tour of duty, towards the early sixties, I began to feel a bit restless. Comfortable though life was working for one of the best employers, where I had made a good impression, and with Sim telling me that if I carried on just as I was and didn't blot my copybook, I would be occupying his Chair as No 1 one day, there was the nagging thought that was I destined to live in Calcutta until the age of 52. Also, would Andrew Yules remain the same as now when you could enjoy six months' leaves without worrying whether your desk would be there on return, or wondering what was happening back at the ranch, as is the constant thought with executives on holiday these days? Nehru's socialist policies could also lead to the nationalisation of such companies, and although not exactly foreseen at the time, this is exactly what happened in 1972 when his daughter, Mrs Gandhi legislated a wave of nationalisation engulfing all banks and Andrew Yules (plus abolishing the Privy Purses and privileges of the Indian Princes, although this had been enshrined in the Indian constitution framed in 1949). Somewhere in the late 1970s the Indian government converted its property in South Audley Street into a Nehru Centre. Rather arrogantly and somewhat stupidly it asked people like Lord Catto (the 2nd Baron) to contribute. At the annual Andrew Yule reunion cocktail party held in the Oriental Club that year, Stephen Catto (the 2nd Baron) asked me if I had been asked to contribute to be told that I had dropped the appeal letter straight into the waste paper basket. In his case, he had replied that if they would return the shareholders' money lost in the nationalisation, he might consider making a contribution.

When I had made up my mind, I advised Sim's (by now Sir Alexander Sim) successor David Macmillan of my decision to resign, and have not forgotten that in his response he was kind enough to say he was heartbroken as I would have had a good innings there. Regrets for some time to come were inevitable on my part, because colleagues had become dear friends, the atmosphere blissfully clear of the backbiting and office politics so endemic in large firms, the usual office monotony reduced by the anticipation and enjoyment of six months' leaves, as well as the transfers from one department to another which were part of the career planning to ensure that you had experience in all the firm's activities by the time you arrived at a position of responsibility.

I would not like to cheat the reader by omitting to recall one episode when I was in the Tea Department. Head Office 'wallahs' like myself were expected to 'inspect' various tea gardens which we managed. The managers and assistants were invariably Scottish; indeed for the jute mills it was company policy not to employ anyone in a managerial capacity if they had been born south of Dundee. I went up to Mim Tea Garden near Darjeeling, and at a height of over 7000 feet it was the highest garden under our management, producing green tea which fetched the highest possible prices at the Tea Auctions in London's Mincing Lane. I was staying at the manager's bungalow with Mr Patterson, a cheerful Scot, who was on his last tour of duty after almost 25 years service in India. His wife had gone home before him. In the customary way, the bungalow was beautifully situated on a spur with lovely views of the Himalayas all around, it was large and comfortable with an army of servants. Although up country managers deferred to Head Office in all matters, their living conditions were superior to those of their bosses in Calcutta. Patterson should have called me either Mr Saroop or Sir, but I allowed him to call me 'Laddie' – he was after all 30 years older. After an excellent dinner, we sat on his wide verandah looking at the stars and faraway twinkling lights of Darjeeling, sipping a post-prandial whisky and soda. Naturally, he was knowledgeable about local history and customs, one of which would be the dream of any schoolboy, probably any normal male. The female tea garden labour from a particular hill tribe made their men very comfortable and prevented any exertion on their part by sitting astride them with no movement on either partner's part except the internal contraction and expansion of their vaginal muscles which eventually bought this delightful game to its climax. I couldn't help thinking that the reclining chairs on which we were sitting with broad arm rests capable of being extended into foot rests were ideal for this type of exercise. There was mutual sadness when I parted from Andrew Yules.

There was a decade or so subsequently of working as a subsidiary company director with two multinationals of the time, Davy Ashmore Group and the Turner & Newall Group, the leading world giant in the Asbestos industry, recently fallen victim to the asbestos lobby. Although both were agreeable, after Yules they were dull. The ethos was different and one's colleagues were not quite from the same stable. It is remarkable that I cannot recall one single incident or episode from my working life during this period that would merit retelling. The same would more or less apply to the corresponding social and sporting life, with one exception.

I was based in Frankfurt for a few months, and was a member of the Kronberg Golf Club, the course winding its way around Schloss Kronberg which had been built by the Kaiser to keep his English mother, Queen Victoria's eldest child, away from the German court. We had an inter-club fixture to play against the Baden-Baden Golf Club on their lovely course, near that beautiful city. I was lucky enough to be selected, and our team were staying at the excellent Hotel Brenners Park, both the hotel and the town reminding me so nostalgically of Simla. Some wives came with the team, and one or two unattached enthusiasts who joined as spectators. One of these was a beautiful Danish lady, erstwhile Denmark's female tennis champion, who had unwisely left her English husband, the heir to a Dukedom, and who lived in Frankfurt with a rich Austrian whose father had started the Austrian Bank, Kreditanstalt. Helmut was away from Frankfurt, so Moody came on her own, and was seated next to me at the team dinner in the hotel's enchanting restaurant. The predictable end to the evening was never in any doubt, but Moody found the dinner boring. I whispered that I too would like to leave as soon as possible, but I was considering her reputation if we left together and too soon. Although the meal was almost over, she suddenly left. While the men at the table were indulging in hearty German humour, 'Why has she left you, why is Herr Saroop looking so?' a waiter came to me, and said there was a phone call for me. There were leers and laughter when I left the table for the telephone kiosk near the reception, and Moody told me on the telephone that if I didn't come up immediately, she was locking her room door. All former and serving cavalry officers will know that in such situations, there is not a moment to lose. An instantaneous decision is required to order advance and charge, with military training almost dictating the use of one's initiative and damn the consequences. When I returned to the concierge's desk in the early hours of the morning to collect my own room key, one of our team called Haberman, head of Daimler-Benz, was wandering around, blind drunk. Spotting me, he put both his hands on my shoulders, and said, 'We all like you, Herr Saroop, but tonight you haf not a good thing done,' before collapsing on the carpet. Some concern about the consequences, combined with only two hours sleep should not have helped my golf the next morning, but such is the quirkiness and unpredictability of the game that I played one of my best rounds ever, achieving hooks and slices on the fairways when I wanted them, and sinking impossible putts from all angles and lengths, and winning my singles match with the last putt on the last green. Returning to the Club House for lunch and expecting to be lionised, I realised that my team were cutting and ignoring me, the Baden-Baden team and my partner from my team in the afternoon being the only ones talking to me. He was Ernest Stinnes, it being said in Germany that what Krupps is to steel, Stinnes is to coal, and had become a friend. Again, I managed to play well, my partner got a hole in one, and we won our match. His parting remark, 'If you need any help, talk to me before the Committee sends for you,' only increased the sinking uneasy feeling in my stomach.

Two days after returning to Frankfurt, the Club Secretary, Herr Winkler, telephoned me to say the Committee liked me, my fellow members liked me, he liked me, I played good golf, but in Baden-Baden 'you have not a good thing done.' He offered me the choice of either outright resignation or facing the Club Court of Honour, which is a custom peculiar to Germany. On the appointed evening, with butterflies in my stomach, I arrived to face what could have been described as a 'we haf vays to make you ...' situation. Seated were Herr Hauer, the President of the Club and a few others, while I was kept standing. They were icily polite, repeated how much I was liked etc., but in Baden-Baden 'you haf not a good thing done.'

'But may I please be told exactly what I did?'

'Ach so, you do not know. You left the President's table at dinner, did not return to say goodnight.'

'If that is all I'm accused of, Herr President and all else have my unqualified apologies.'

'Ach so, you apologise? The matter is then settled.'

I didn't need a lawyer, I was on the wrong charge, and as they often do, the Germans had completely missed the point.

8

Notting Hill and Party Games

Residents, visitors and aficionados of the film 'Notting Hill' would not have recognised it in the 1970s. The area was badly run down, there were slummy bed sits, and almost every nationality under the sun was represented there. Parts of it were almost no-go areas, particularly in the run up to the Notting Hill Carnival which had already become an annual fixture over the August Bank Holiday weekend. Almost every nationality had its own Committee leading to a plethora of organisations, each claiming to speak for all, although most of the time each spokesman represented mainly himself or herself. They had grand-sounding names like 'International Organisation for Overseas Moroccans', or the 'Union of Muslim Organisations of UK and Eire', the latter never disclosing how many members they actually had in Ireland. Each had plenty of soap box politicians vociferously criticising all authority, but yet demanding more and more handouts, particularly from their local Council, the Royal Borough of Kensington and Chelsea. Nobody has been able to come to a definitive conclusion about the Reds under the Bed scare and conspiracy theory of the 1960s and 1970s, but I can say from personal experience in Notting Hill that there were many individuals there, with no known employment or source of income, who were paid by different Communist parties around the world. Their brief was to create as much confusion and chaos as they could, to probe for weak spots in local authority organisations which frequently gave in because they lacked the firmness to stand fast. Each surrender meant further demands, with councillors and chairmen of various committees being bullied and hectored until some lost their nerve.

A kind friend, now Sir Michael Craig-Cooper, to whom I owe much, advised me that it would be no bad idea to get a bit of local government experience, and to put my name forward to succeed him as one of the councillors for Hans Town Ward (comprising the jungles and wildernesses of the area around Harrods, and perhaps the safest Tory ward in the whole country). Michael was himself being appointed an Alderman, and the majority Tory party on the Council was full of a lot of talent and experience, our then Chief Whip Joan Hanham being now in the House of Lords. Notwithstanding the frustration of being in perpetual opposition, the Labour side on the Council also had a number of able people, their leaders being the Hon. Thomas Ponsonby, popularly known as the Hon. Tom Pon, going to the Lords on his father's death. The Council Leader, the senior Tory, was Sir Malby Crofton Bt, for whom I developed much affection and respect. The regeneration of North Kensington, which includes Notting Hill, was conceived, planned and implemented by him with missionary zeal, and he has received insufficient credit and recognition for laying the seeds to make the area north of Bayswater Road look as it now does. One of his original ideas, reputed to be the first time it has been tried out in the western world was to use the empty derelict space under the M40 motorway in its very early stages as it passes through the Royal Borough. Some of it was thereby used for shops, small-scale businesses or industrial units, and to establish a mini Town Hall obviating the requirement for the old and the needy to travel much further to the main Town Hall in Kensington High Street for advice and assistance. I think we also involved the North Kensington Amenity Trust. Malby, even more than others, recognised the need also for better community relations in the area, but to be achieved realistically, and not by bribing them with more and more money, which was generally wasted. He and I had several conversations before my election in May 1974, and it was agreed that I would be the Chairman of the yet to be formed Borough Community Relations Committee, further agreeing that initially it should have the extremely modest annual budget of no more than £1000, thereby enabling me to say with my hand on my heart that I had no more to give away when hectored by undeserving causes. There was many a time once we had got going when a self-appointed spokesman for some organisation or the other would say to me, 'I am not going to discuss anything with you, as you have no money to give away,' and my response was that he could please himself, and could he inform his community that therefore they didn't want to be represented on the Community Relations Committee. Without exception, all of them came back.

The prevailing national pattern of the time was that in the relevant areas, a Borough Community Relations Council was set up under the aegis of the newly-established Race Relations Board, which financed them, thereby more or less obliging them to follow a general policy framework laid down by itself. In principle, there was, and is, nothing wrong with this, but it did mean that you couldn't stop hotheads and troublemakers from becoming a part of it, thereby in some cases vitiating the very purpose i.e. of communal harmony and of having a local Borough Community Relations unit. Malby and I were determined that the Royal Borough would not be influenced by the national pattern, that we would pursue the objective of harmonious community relations on our own, more realistically. This was one reason why we called ours a Committee and not Council, as was the national pattern. Soon enough there were the expected reactions. The troublemakers showered the local press with accusations that the Royal Borough Council was being authoritarian by not doing what everybody else did, and we received a letter from the Race Relations Board requiring an explanation. I had to go to a meeting with their Chairman, Mark Bonham-Carter. He couldn't understand why the Royal Borough was the only local authority in the country which for years had not had a Community Relations Council, and when it finally did, it was defying the pattern. This meant that he couldn't allot us any money from his budget, which we didn't want anyway. His irritation showed, but we parted amicably.

But there were other fun and games afoot. There was a disused and deconsecrated church called the Talbot Tabernacle, which the Council had purchased with the intention of renovating it into a Community Centre and handing it over to the local organisations to do with as they pleased, plus a dowry of £100,000 to get it on its way. To bring this about we set up a Talbot Tabernacle Working Group, to which all groups were invited to send representatives, with myself as the Chairman and one of the Council Officers as Clerk to the Committee. What should have been easily decided and resolved in two or three meetings took over seven months, with disruptive behaviour leading to some meetings lasting until past midnight.

It was this involvement that gave me an insight into Communist tactics. They first said that £100,000 was insufficient. It took three meetings for them to accept that I was not going to budge. The next tactic was to roundly abuse the poor Clerk that the Minutes were not accurate, and shouting at me for signing them as correct. A number of them said, 'I spoke for over half an hour at the last meeting, not a word has been recorded, and my supporters don't believe that I am voicing their views.' The Chairman's reply was that according to Council procedure, we only recorded decisions taken. Then there was the scramble for places on the Executive Committee of the new Community Centre. This led to many rowdy scenes, with the police having to be called on one occasion. We seemed to be getting nowhere, when one of their number asked for a private meeting with me. This gentleman was Bruno Pallotta, an Italian reputedly being financed by the Communist Party of his homeland, who had materialised in the Borough out of nowhere. He was a perfectly amiable chap, and gave me excellent advice. 'Councillor, why don't you follow the Chinese Communist pattern, put everyone who wishes it on the Executive Committee; they will feel important, but set up a small Consultative Committee which will really make the decisions.' I did just that, and we cleared that hurdle. The final hurdle was the numerous conflicting opinions about what to call the new Centre. This was the rowdiest meeting of the whole series. After several adjournments, they advised me that they had unanimously agreed to call it 'The Moscow Centre'.

'I can't accept that,' was the Chairman's answer.

'Why not?' was the loud noise.

'Because this is not Moscow.'

'In that case, we walk out.'

'You are entitled to do so, but the Council will carry on with its plans.'

'Well then you suggest an acceptable name.'

'I have three from which you can take your pick. The first is Queen Elizabeth the Second's Her Majesty Centre in North Kensington, the second is Councillor Sir Malby Crofton Centre, and the third and last is Councillor Major Saroop Centre.' There were hoots of derisive laughter, shouting and banging, but finally it was agreed to call it the Talbot Centre. When it was all over, some of them, including Signor Pallotta, very kindly and generously said to me, 'Councillor, you didn't give us all we wanted, all we thought we could get away with, but you were fair.' It's one of the best compliments I've had; Pallotta then disappeared as mysteriously as he had arrived, presumably to go and create trouble elsewhere if he could find a softer touch.

There was another amusing incident. Shortly after we had commissioned the mini Town Hall under the Motorway, the police telephoned one evening to advise me the gypsies were squatting there, and I told them to also inform the Chairman of the Social Services Committee, Councillor Mrs Jocelyn Sundies-Smith, a doughty formidable daughter of the Empire, and a lady like a galleon in full sail. She was an Army daughter, managing to escape just in time from Hong Kong when the Japs came in in 1941. We met in the besieged and occupied premises, with the police already there.

Jocelyn and I agreed that we would spend the night there, if necessary, to assert Council ownership, and so we did in our respective sleeping bags. The local press produced a juicy headline the next day, 'Two Councillors spend night together', but they did not quote in my own statement, 'Councillor Sundies-Smith is the best example of a daughter of the Empire; I am an honourable former Regular Cavalry officer; how dare you impute that anything improper could have taken place, particularly as we were surrounded by all manner of gypsies'.

At the time, the Notting Hill Carnival also fell partly in my areas of responsibility, and I used to dread the August Bank Holiday weekend, with nasty incidents every year. All these were law and order problems, to be dealt with by the police, but this did not stop troublemakers telephoning me at all hours over the weekend. After two or three years of this, my wife and I arranged to be away each year to stay with Sir Robert Throckmorton at his estate in North Devon, if only to remind ourselves of the contrast with Notting Hill. In the interest of the poor residents in the affected streets, I have always publicly stated that the Carnival should be held elsewhere, like Hyde Park Corner.

For some time now I had been thinking about ways and means of attracting Asian voters to the Tory Party, as with very few exceptions they were all in the Labour fold. One of the ideas suggested by Conservative Central Office was to start a newspaper aimed at them; but in which language? There were Punjabis, Gujarati, Bangladeshis, each with a different language. The natural choice of English was ruled out because at the time their population consisted mainly of first generation immigrants with scant knowledge of English. It was finally decided to follow my suggestion to establish an Anglo-Asian Conservative Society, which would have branches in the relevant constituencies. To forestall any criticism that the move could be divisive, inasmuch as why didn't Asians with Tory sympathies join their local Conservative Associations anyway, I announced that the Society should be seen as a temporary bridge, to enable the Asians and the local Tories to meet halfway. It has to be said to our shame that at the time there were a number of constituencies where the local Tories did not welcome Asian members, who were therefore reluctant and shy to come forward. Time and increased contact through the Society would wear down reservations on both sides, and that would be the time to blow up the temporary bridge. The Press made much of it, mainly snide; the Labour Party were taken by surprise and envy that they had been gazumped about something which they had not had the courage to do themselves; enlightened Tories who included most of the higher echelons of the Tory Party were delighted, and those not so enlightened, were cynical about the whole project hiding behind the argument that this would upset white Tory voters. It has to be said that colour prejudice was definitely prevalent in certain sections of the Party. Mrs Thatcher was not entirely enthusiastic either, but was finally persuaded by the likes of Lords Home and Glendevon (the younger son of a former Viceroy of India, Lord Linlithgow), who took a long term view of things and without whose help and influence the Society would never have got off the ground. It was a few years later when Tories were in office that, in some context or the other, Lord Home remarked to me, 'My dear boy, did you know that the Prime Minister has never read a history book in her life?'

It was decided to launch the Society in the Smith Square premises of Conservative Central Office, with Willie Whitelaw as the Shadow Home Secretary and David Lane, MP, who was or had been on the Race Relations Board, to support me. The Press had been invited, Tory MPs sympathetic to the cause, and like-minded Asians from around the country for the event due to take place in a large basement room. We did apprehend that the National Front and similar would probably create a fuss, and we were right. On the appointed morning I could see about a dozen National Front people with placards and banners, all saying more or less 'Deportation is the answer to immigration.' I chose my target, wondering how and where the Front had managed to recruit the pleasant comely girl performing her duties with enthusiasm. Looking straight into her eyes, making sure the TV cameras were on me – something at which years later Princess Diana was at her manipulative best – I asked her where would she deport me. 'I don't mean you at all,' she stammered. The hall inside also had a number of the Front Rent-a-Mob, led by the Dowager Lady Birdwood with her chief acolyte, a matron from a West London Hospital. The first Lord Birdwood, a Field Marshal had been Commander-in-Chief in India in the 1930s. His son, the second Lord Birdwood had married a daughter of Sir George Drummond Ogilvie who had been Defence Secretary in Delhi, and whose son Alec Ogilvie had been one of the 'burra sahibs' or my chief in Andrew Yule's in Calcutta. I remember his distress when he received the news that Birdwood had left his sister to marry the children's nanny, and the latter as the second Lady Birdwood was the one I was now confronting. There was heckling and shouting, with Lady Birdwood stating that '... it was disgraceful that the Tory Party was encouraging Asians to join it, when it is a well known fact that the incidence of tuberculosis had significantly increased in areas like Southall after Punjabi immigrants settled there, and here is a local matron by my side to substantiate it.'

David Lane asked me, in the Chair, to rule it out of order. I said that I would rather reply. 'Lady Birdwood,' I said, 'perhaps you do not know that your late husband used to stay with my family in the Punjab during the War on his recruiting drives, and those that he recruited, fought valiantly for the Crown in Burma, North Africa and Italy. Some of them, and their close kith and kin are the very people you now accuse. Your husband would have been ashamed of your conduct here today; and what is more, it is a well known historical, medical and military fact that there was no venereal disease in the sylvan surroundings of the Simla Hills with its beautiful local women until British troops were first stationed there in the 1840s.' Lady Birdwood stood up and shouted, 'Mr Whitelaw, this is utterly disgraceful. I demand that this meeting be stopped immediately.'

'I can't, Lady Birdwood, I'm not in the Chair,' replied Willie.

Shortly after the General Election of 1979 I had another idea, which was to start a new dining club for the emerging financial leaders of the Asian community, with the object of providing a forum for them to meet their counterparts in the social and business strata in the UK, and also to provide electoral and financial help to the Tory Party; there were then, and still are, a number of dining Clubs of this nature e.g. the United and Cecil, the 1900 and so on, but the Asians were still a bit shy and reluctant to come forward to join them. The new Club would provide them with a sort of cocoon where they could feel comfortable with more of their own kind. Once again, Alec Home and John Glendevon were a great help, and after a number of jolly discussions, we agreed on a name for it – The Durbar Club, which has the right ring about it, the word Durbar being an Urdu word – in different context, it can mean a court, a throne, or even the person occupying the throne. The Prime Minister or Leader of the Party, as the case may be, would be its Patron, and the incumbent Chairman of the Party, its President, with myself as the Chairman. This has continued to this day, but in the beginning we were fortunate to have two Patrons, Alec Home and Margaret Thatcher, to be succeeded in turn by John Major, William Hague and Iain Duncan-Smith, and now Michael Howard. In its heyday in the 1980s and mid 1990s, the Club used to have four or five dinners a year, always with a distinguished speaker as Chief Guest, and in that period there was not a single Cabinet Minister who had not dined with the Club. We were also extremely fortunate in being able to hold our functions in locations like 12 Downing Street, the Chief Whip's premises, 1 Carlton Gardens which is the Foreign Secretary's London residence, in the Commons and the Lords, in my own Clubs in the West End, and Livery Halls in the City. Our chief guests and speakers were not always political; they included the Archbishop of Canterbury, Commissioner of Scotland Yard, Chairmen of the CBI and the Institute of Directors, the Government's Chief Scientific Adviser, Chairman of the BBC, and so on. It was at one of these functions in Draper's Hall per courtesey of

Michael Craig-Cooper, that on behalf of the Club, my wife presented a cheque for £110,000 to Mrs Thatcher to pay for the installation of the very first computer equipment at Conservative Central Office.

One evening our guest was Michael Heseltine who had recently taken over as Secretary of State for Defence. 'What would you like me to speak on, Narindar?' he queried. The answer was to make it something personal, as all our speakers were requested to do, rather than a politician's speech. He came up trumps, saying 'Gentlemen, when I walked into the office of my new responsibilities, there was the usual line of secretaries assembled there; there was the Permanent Secretary, my personal secretary, my diary secretary and so on. A brief scene of Yes Minister, No Minister ensued. I held up my hand, and asked them to leave me alone as I wanted to think. After they had reluctantly withdrawn, I tried to think of something to show them who was really in command; I put my feet on my desk, summoned them back to announce that I didn't like the way in which the furniture and pictures are arranged in this room. Let us spend the rest of the morning getting it rearranged.' His withdrawal from frontline politics, due to his illness, was a serious loss to the Party and country, and particularly so because of the time it happened.

The Durbar Club also used to arrange a reception at each Party Conference to which the great and good always came. In 1984, it was held in one of the ground floor rooms in the Grand Hotel, Brighton. For reasons to become rather poignant a few hours later, I particularly remember one incident. Guests had come and gone, there were a few people left, when the Hon. Anthony Berry, MP came back a second time. He had been our Parliamentary Whip for the London Parliamentary Candidates Association, and was a very likeable fellow. He had his son with him, wanted to introduce him to Willie Whitelaw in case he was still at our reception, but I said he had just left. That was the last time I saw Tony Berry. After dinner, my wife and I returned to the small country hotel near Lewes where we were staying. Disaster struck; I had forgotten our key, and there was nobody around until the first member of staff arrived around 6 a.m., with my poor wife and I having to make do with the sofas in the Drawing Room. Breakfast in the room, and a brief fitful doze later, I telephoned the Grand Hotel to tell them I would be looking in at lunchtime to collect Durbar Club bits and pieces left behind, and to settle my account. There was a pause the other end, and the Reception Manager then said, 'But Mr Saroop, have you not heard?' It was then that we heard about the previous night's bomb. Tony Berry was one of the fatal casualties.

The Anglo-Asian Conservative Society has undergone a series of name changes since I gave up as Founder Chairman in 1987, some of these including 'Outreach', 'Contact', 'Connect' and other such esoterics which I'm sure are understood by the people who thought of them. The Durbar Club is not as active as it used to be, but is a sleeper, to be reactivated when the Party is back in office. In not exploiting to the full the potential of these two assets which I was privileged enough to create, this self-inflicted wound continues to damage the Party, electorally and financially.

9
A Hookah and a Hunt Ball

'Tories choose Englishman from the Punjab', were the thick headlines on Page 5 in the issue of 14th October 1975 of The Daily Telegraph. It went on to say that Mr Saroop had been selected the previous evening by the Greenwich Conservative Association to fight the Parliamentary seat at the next General Election, and that I was the Tory Party's first ever Indian Parliamentary candidate.

I was quoted correctly as saying that I was as happy smoking a Hookah under a tree as I was at a Hunt Ball – only to learn a few days later that this remark had not quite pleased the then Chairman of the Party, Lord Thorneycroft. 'Rubbish', said some of my friends at the time, 'Saroop cannot manage to sit cross-legged, and the only Hookah he can recognise is a Havana cigar.' Peter never said anything to me, but I quite understood his dilemma then with the Party, mistakenly, wanting to distance itself from Hunt Balls, but not being able to quite make up its mind about how to respond to the Hookah. It still has not done so, and has suffered and continues to suffer electorally for mistakes made by Mrs Thatcher, who in the sixteen years in command intransigently refused to address the issue, notwithstanding numerous prods from Lord Home, Lord Glendevon who was the senior-most Privy Councillor at the time, and numerous other senior Tory Party figures. A number of the top Tories at the time, and later, told me that she tended to judge many issues from the lower middle class yardstick of how it would all appear in Grantham. Poor John Major and William Hague had to carry the can on this issue, but Michael Howard has seriously addressed it. None of them is to blame, but the Party has missed the boat in attracting Asian voters, of which more later.

There was a spate of letters the following day from Mr Know-All, Sir Know-All and Lord Know-All around the country ticking off the newspaper, since Sir Manakjee Bhavnagri had sat as a Tory MP from 1896 to 1906 for Bethnal Green East; now that was a well-ordered world when Bethnal Green returned a Tory to the Commons. The poor chap was thrown out in 1906, along with most of the other Tories in an election as disastrous for us as the one in 1997. However, all the know-alls were unanimous in agreeing that it would be perfectly correct to describe Mr Saroop as the Tory Party's first Indian Parliamentary Candidate in the 20th century. To my dismay, the media soon changed the Indian to Asian, and there was nothing I could do to change or stop it. I am proud of my ancestry, and not exactly enamoured of polyglot societies like America or Singapore.

Getting selected for Greenwich was fun. At the time I was short-listed for the constituencies of Hammersmith North and Holborn and St Pancras. All were near unwinnable seats, short of a miracle. The call to Greenwich came earlier than the other two. By that time, I had a bit of experience about these events, but only those who have been through the procedure would be able to fully appreciate all that it entails.

The aspirant has to apply to be put on the Approved Tory Parliamentary Candidates List, only after which can he or she apply for various constituencies. At this time, the applicant had to be sponsored by two MPs. I was fortunate enough to have the late Julian Amery and Patrick McNair-Wilson as my supporters. After this you were expected to do some work in a toughish constituency – my home constituency of Chelsea did not fall in that category – before an interview with a Panel of two or three MPs who had the final say. The exact name of the North London constituency where I was deputed to help escapes me, but it later became

Ken Livingstone territory. The Constituency Agent was a jolly young man, and the Parliamentary Candidate was the late George Young, ex-Deputy Head of MI6.

The first evening I visited the Constituency Offices, I almost crashed into a Rolls being driven out of the short drive. Somebody shouted 'Oh, my God, you almost killed George Young'. A few moments later I told the agent that I had not realized that our Parliamentary candidate had a Rolls. 'Don't be bloody silly, that was George Young the builder, George Young the candidate drives a clapped-out Mini', was the answer. The latter became a friend, and one day when I mentioned to him that life was a bit dull in his constituency, he said, 'Well, Narindar, let's go and stir up some trouble somewhere else.'

In my efforts to help the Conservative Association there, I was fortunate enough to call on the help of two friends, the late Jack di Manio, well-known to all wireless listeners, and the late Desmond Donnelly, former MP for Pembroke. For the Jack di Manio evening, we sold around 30 tickets at £3.00 each raising £90.00 for the Party, considered a bit of a record in the Constituency annals. Desmond was a most talented person, a senior respected Labour politician, who disliked Harold Wilson's mendacity, and made the unfortunate decision to start a new political party, losing Pembroke to Nick Edwards in the process. On the evening he had come, at my request, to speak in the constituency we eventually ended up at his Club, the Royal Air Force in Piccadilly, where we bumped into a former Air Commodore and about to retire Tory MP. I can't remember his name, but he buttonholed Donnelly and said, 'Desmond, I hear you are trying to get back into the House; don't be mad, it's now a madhouse.' Desmond pointed to me, and said he should talk to me as I was trying to get in for the first time. The Air Commodore very kindly offered me a drink, and trying to dissuade me said, 'When I got into the Commons in the '45 General Election, and feeling my way around the place, I ran into a senior Tory member moderately inebriated. He was wandering around, saying that everything was awful. I asked him why, getting the reply that he had to face his constituents the next day, and what was worse, was that he was obliged to do the same next year. Wasn't it awful?' Having said that, the Air Commodore said to me, 'You see, my boy, don't you? It's not the place it was. By the time you get in, you may have to face your constituents three or four times a year.'

Desmond's defection to the Tories provided the Party with a public relations coup, but did not help poor Desmond. Although people like Willie Whitelaw kept on muttering that the Party must find him a seat, Desmond was not even called to make a speech at that year's Party Conference, although he had been assured by Whitelaw that he would be, as a sort of first step to get constituencies to look at his candidature. Reg Prentice was more successful at about the same time, getting in as a Tory MP for one if not two terms. Desmond found life stacking up against him; having written successful books on contemporary politics and having a daily column in a national newspaper, he saw them evaporating as his remaining source of income. It was with considerable sadness that I read the news of his suicide on the tape one afternoon in 1977 or 1978. He had booked a room at the Airport Hotel on the M4 near Heathrow, locked the door and taken an overdose. At his memorial service later in St Margaret's, Westminster, Whitelaw gave a moving address which to me sounded hollow. I told him after the service that the Party should have done more to help Desmond. 'I know we killed him, Narindar, we killed him,' said Willie. Donnelly deserved better all round.

Having managed to set up one or two Ward Committees in a rather apathetic constituency, I requested a meeting with Bill Elliott, now Lord Elliott of Morpeth who was at the time the Party Vice-Chairman in charge of candidates, suggesting rather cheekily that it was about time that I was included in the Approved List of Candidates. A less kindly man than Bill would have thrown me out, advised or instructed me to acquire more political experience by working in places like the Gorbals etc. etc. However, Bill allowed me to move to the final stage of the interview with the Parliamentary Panel, where I must have managed not to upset anybody because shortly afterwards a letter arrived advising that my name was now on the Approved List. Constituencies wishing to choose a Parliamentary Candidate ask Central Office for names to interview, the constituency's name is circulated to all those on the List, and those interested then put their names forward, with the Constituency Association then deciding which ones to interview, propose a short list of three or four depending on their own rules, enabling them to make the final selection. Anybody interested locally can apply direct to the Association without having to be on the List. Those standing out for the first time are unlikely to be interviewed for a safe or winnable constituency, convention having laid down that they must first undergo battle inoculation for at least one election in hopeless seats, fighting awesome majorities against them.

The first constituency for which I applied was Birmingham Sparkbrook in a Don Quixote gesture to take on Roy Hattersley for the February 1974 Election, and was overjoyed to receive a letter from them saying I had been short-listed, and naming a time in the evening of the date for the interview; if married, one was expected to bring one's wife so that your potential electors could delight, in addition to making you feel uncomfortable, in a critical appraisal of your wife's clothes, and ogle her if she were attractive. My poor devoted wife who certainly fell in that category endured a number of such interviews for my sake, subsequently being very loyal and hardworking when we were both nursing Greenwich. I still don't know exactly when it became the vogue that constituents demand and require the poor MP's wife, or rather the MP's poor wife, to share his constituency burdens and responsibilities. It is certainly not chivalrous, if anyone understands the word these days, it is certainly demeaning, and probably also between unkind and cruel. If so, the constituents' fire is misdirected. By all means, if you so mistakenly wish, be unkind to your MP, but why expect his loyal wife to participate in constituency burdens? Perhaps the whole thing will die a natural or unnatural death when partners, no longer wives, of MPs like Peter Mandelson will refuse to accept these procedures.

We left London early on the appointed day for the meeting at 7 pm in a school hall in Birmingham, looking in on the way to lunch followed by tea at Coughton Court, the centuries old ancestral seat of the Throckmortons, about half an hour's drive from our destination that evening. Sir Robert very kindly armed me with a pork pie and a small flask of whisky 'to give you strength to speak well', he said, while saying farewell. Arriving on a cold, misty evening in the school courtyard, the evening could not have been more dismal, perhaps a portent of my later fate. The only other candidate on the short list was Andrew McKay, now in the House of Commons. He and his wife were interviewed first, giving me time to have a bite and a swig at the Throckmorton supplies. Procedures at these meetings can vary slightly, but the form that evening was that the candidate should speak for ten or fifteen minutes on a subject of his own choosing, followed by a question and answer free for all of a similar duration. I do not know what inspired me to choose as my subject 'The Pursuit of Excellence'. It was not a wise choice. The Chairman of the meeting was Hon Alderman Chamberlain. I forget his first name, but he was a nephew of the late Prime Minister, Neville Chamberlain. There were no more than five or six dear old ladies in the large hall, and as my wife told me later that one of them was knitting, while the others were deeply absorbed in the antics of a hamster resident in the classroom. I thought I delivered my speech well, and the time came for questions, answers and discussion. Dead silence! After the third time that the Hon Alderman had said 'Any questions?' it soon became clear that there were not going to be any. Some embarrassing moments later I was thanked, and my wife and I were asked to join the waiting McKays. He and I did a quick post-mortem and reading between the lines it emerged that each would be rather relieved if the other got the constituency. Some time later, the Chairman emerged to say 'I have to announce that our Selection Committee has chosen Mr Mckay as our Parliamentary Candidate, and I would like him and his wife to come back to the Hall and speak to them again. If Mr Saroop would be so kind as to wait, I would appreciate a word with him before departure.' He could not have been kinder or better intentioned when he returned and said, 'Mr Saroop, I understand that this is your first constituency interview. I congratulate you on your talk, but is the pursuit of excellence quite the subject to choose for Birmingham? I was the only one there who understood a word you said. No wonder there were no questions. I wish you good luck in your search for a constituency.'

After Sparkbrook there were one or two other interviews over a stretch of time ending in another abortive attempt at Eton and Slough, where I realised later that I had already unwittingly antagonised the Selection Committee. A few days prior to this interview, a well-known political columnist of The Times called George Hutchinson had written as follows: '... The Tories in Eton and Slough with its large Asian population will be mad not to seize on Narindar Saroop as an almost ideal candidate to oust the sitting Labour MP, Miss Joan Lestor ...' George meant well, and was giving me a helping hand. On the day it appeared, 8th December 1973, I walked into the Carlton Club rather jauntily for lunch, only to have my smugness dented by the general comment: 'George's comments have made Narindar's friends happy, made him happy, made certain sections of Conservative Central Office happy, but the people probably made rather unhappy are the Selection Committee you are going to face shortly'. That was the end of Eton and Slough.

The beginning for Greenwich came some time later. One morning the usual letter, the type of which I had become a near veteran of receiving, arrived from the Greenwich Conservative Association saying that after an earlier preliminary interview they had short-listed me with three other candidates, and advising me of the date and time in the evening for the final selection interview. It was to follow the usual drill of a ten minute speech, followed by questions and discussion, but it was specified that in common with other candidates I could speak on any subject of my choice. I wrestled in my mind for several days, right until lunchtime on the appointed day, but couldn't really make up my mind about what to say. With her usual concern and loyalty, my wife repeatedly asked me in the intervening time if I had worked on my speech. An accidental meeting in the Members' Room at the Carlton Club proves the old theory that quite often the best things happen by chance. After lunch, preoccupied and increasingly worried, I almost stumbled over the semi-recumbent distinguished form of Sir William Teeling, formerly Member for Brighton Hove or Pavilion, and whom I had first met in Ireland years ago, when he had a charming house on the edge of Phoenix Park to be sold later to become the residence of the Italian Ambassador in Dublin.

'I'm frightfully sorry, Sir William,' I apologised.

'Is it about that bloody awful tie you are wearing?' said he.

I looked at my tie, looked perfectly respectable to me, he motioned me to sit in the chair next to him, and I blurted out about the selection that evening, and I just couldn't think of what to say.

'Japan, dear boy, talk about Japan', was Sir William's advice. 'When I was selected for Brighton I spoke about Japan.'

'Obviously you knew a great deal about it,' I said.

'Nothing, never been there in my life. But neither had they.'

I pondered over this seriously for the rest of the afternoon, collected my wife, and we drove to Greenwich through places which had until then been just names on a London Bus – Clapham, Peckham, Streatham, Lewisham and so on. In transit through Streatham, Duncan-Sandy's words came back to me. His constituents in Streatham voiced their concern that they didn't see their MP often enough, if at all, to be met by the riposte, 'You sent me to the Commons to represent Streatham; surely you don't want me here to represent the Commons.' It was about this time that my wife enquired again whether I had decided what I was going to say. I said I had, but couldn't tell her, because the remaining time was too short to listen to it, and analyse and discuss it. She has always been the best judge of my speeches, always commenting most helpfully on their content, and any over-abundant signs of arrogance and conceit. 'Well, it's your funeral', she said, as we drove into the car park of the Greenwich Conservative Area offices, or rather of the local Conservative Club being used that evening. One of the other candidates was Alderman Arthur Rolfe, who had served on the Borough Council for many years, had tried for the Parliamentary seat at least twice before, and was determined to succeed this time, and having considerable support in the local Conservative Association he was the strong local candidate, according to the briefing I had had from Central Office. I can't remember in which order the candidates were called in, there are many theories as to the advantages or disadvantages of being called first, second and so on, but I feel it really makes no difference. The tie that you wear or the dress that your wife is wearing can sometimes be a deciding factor. It is arbitrary, haphazard and a lottery and roulette. If your luck is in, you will get it, irrespective of almost everything else. My luck was certainly in that evening.

We were called in, Stephanie hiding her concern at not knowing what I was going to say. I looked at the faces in the room from the platform where the Association Officers and the candidates were seated. They looked a friendly bunch, and I decided to take the plunge. I did have an alternative speech ready, but had decided to choose which one exactly at the last moment. One develops an instinct about audiences; one could guess in the very first few seconds as to which is a possible enemy, which a possible supporter, etc.

'Chairman, Ladies and Gentlemen,' I started off in time honoured fashion, 'you have asked me to speak for fifteen minutes. All I have to say is that Greenwich is the centre of the world, it should therefore be a Tory seat; will you help me to make it so? I have nothing more to say, and this will give you more time to pepper me with questions.' Some time later, the Chairman made the joyous announcement of my selection, and told me privately that the other candidates had rambled on beyond their allotted time, promised to do the un-do-able for Greenwich, about all of which the Selection Committee were highly cynical having heard it time and again from every Tory Candidate over the years. One of the first letters of congratulation and support that I received was from Alderman Arthur Rolfe, which says much for him and for the state of the Tory Party at the time.

On the drive back, and at home I felt I hadn't quite elicited from Stephanie the ecstatic pat on the back I thought I deserved.

'What did you think of my speech?' I asked of my darling.

'The shortest you've ever made; keep them like that, but I'm proud of you.'

10
The 1979 General Election

'If anybody should ask you what are you doing in British politics, tell them the story of that horse; it was a present from your kinsmen,' said Malik Col. Sir Khizar Hyat Tiwana as my car drove him past the equestrian statue of Lord Napier of Magdala which stands at the top end of Queensgate, facing Kensington Gardens. The horse had been gifted by his grandfather to Napier in around 1870 or so, when the latter embarked from Bombay in command of a British Indian force for East Africa to subdue Emperor Theodora of Abyssinia. The horse was named after the victory of Magdala, brought back to India and put out to grass back in the Tiwana lands in the Punjab. Sir Khizar told me that as a young man he remembered one of their Sikh grooms riding the horse round and round their extensive lands, shouting 'Out of my way, out of my way, I am riding the horse on which Lord Napier conquered Africa.' This story circulated in London's Clubland, the well-known columnist, diarist and author Kenneth Ross got hold of it, and wrote about it in The Sunday Telegraph. Inevitably, my leg was pulled by questions about my horse, notwithstanding my protests that I could never afford it, that I'd hardly ever been to a race meeting because I'm not a lucky gambler. However, I still salute the horse twice a day as I pass it from and to home nearby.

One measure, amongst others, of the importance of the Tiwana family was that they were the only hereditary Royal Heralds in

India, selected by Buckingham Palace and the government of the time in the 1860s in preference over the rulers of the vast states like Hyderabad, Kashmir or Patiala. Khizar's grandfather proclaimed Queen Victoria, his father proclaimed King Edward VII and King George V, and Khizar himself would have proclaimed King George VI had a Durbar been held when he became King Emperor. There was a regular cavalry regiment in the Order of Battle in the Indian Army titled 19th King George V's Own Tiwana Lancers, about one-third of its 600 strength being from the Tiwana clan. His father had been India's Agent-General (now called High Commissioner) in London in the 1930s, and was the first occupant of the magnificent India House building in Aldwych. Khizar was the last Premier of undivided Punjab, and practised great affection and loyalty for my grandfather, who had declined the Premiership, and supported Khizar to succeed to the post. We were all related a few centuries ago, as the Tiwanas are fellow Jats who had converted to Islam. Like my grandfather, he had always been against the Partition of India, but sadly accepted that it became inevitable after the Tories lost the 1945 Election. When in London he was often invited to the Churchill residence in Hyde Park Gate, 'next door to my horse', and when he died on his ranch and estate in California in January 1975, I had to go to St James's Palace to report the death of the last Indian hereditary Herald.

Around this time I was working harder than ever before, or since. It was not exactly easy to be earning a living in the City, discharging my responsibilities on the Royal Borough Council, running the Anglo-Asian Conservative Society, and most impor-tantly, 'nursing Greenwich', which was my 'first love' at the time. It would probably be boring for non-political readers to say too much about constituency work as a Parliamentary Candidate or an MP. Unless you like or love people, don't do it. In the words of a former Deputy Chairman of the Party, in whose office I was when he was dealing with his correspondence, he said, 'This is a job for nutters, Narindar, which is what you and I are.' Precisely; politics deals essentially with human nature, is therefore never boring with each day bringing ever changing problems and situations. There is no other walk of life which provides the same variety, and it is therefore not for the faint-hearted; it does not matter whether you are dealing with Defence or Foreign Affairs, rather than social problems; its all to do with the human situation, unlike say in business where one could be tackling production difficulties or the exchange rate and therefore much more circumscribed. With a number of exceptions, a sitting MP is of course in a much easier position than the Parliamentary Candidate trying hard to win the seat, or if unwinnable, to give a good account of himself. Or herself, I should add, pretending to be politically correct.

One of the many excellent courses run by the Industrial Society was on Motivation. Its founder, the late John Garnett, father of Virginia Bottomley, MP, used to say that if we had something interesting to do, we would not find it difficult to jump out of our beds in the mornings, particulary on Mondays. This is exactly how I felt in those exciting years – half a day or more in the City, the rest of the day on Council duties, or in my Constituency, and have never felt more alive. 'Half a day in the City' would raise almost every eyebrow these days. 'It is advisable and desirable,' said many wise friends, 'if not essential to achieve financial independence before going into politics.' This was not so in my case, since really after the debacle of 1947 I had realised that independence was unlikely. But I was fortunate to have employers in Lloyds who were understanding and did not discourage my political involvement, therefore allowing me to enjoy the constituency work. I had said around the time of my adoption that of the three main types of MPs, i.e. a good constituency man, a good House of Commons man, and a Cabinet or higher aspirant, I would like to concentrate on being the first two, as realistically there was never any question of the third.

Greenwich was no exception to the rule that Constituency Associations like to make their MPs and Parliamentary Candidates' life difficult, the latter having to work harder because he has not been elected yet. Door to door canvassing was expected of you every time you were in the constituency, and the Association Officers plus the Agent took perverse delight in sending you off to the most difficult and toughest areas in the constituency, and in the case of Greenwich places where no Tory had ever set foot before. One of these was the almost notorious Ferrier Estate, a vast post-war architectural monstrosity, depressingly visible to all driving to Canterbury or Dover, with some bits of it in my constituency, and the balance in the adjacent seat of Woolwich. It was said that the post-Labour administration deliberately planned this worst example of council housing in order to ensure that Greenwich and Woolwich would never be anything but Labour ever again. It was a depressing, almost hazardous place to canvas, and I learnt two valuable lessons; first that people were surprised that I was surprised to discover how much corruption there was at local levels, and secondly that in various pockets of the country like the Ferrier Estate, my beloved civilised England was no different from gangland Chicago.

A poor old lady living alone greeted me, 'Never seen the likes of you here before,' and poured her heart out about being bullied by a gang of young thugs living with their parents on the Estate. I followed up my promise to do something about it by speaking to the police; they shrugged it off saying that being Greater London Council property, it was private, and a matter for the GLC, who in turn told me that it was a matter for the local residents association, the Chairman of which turned out to be the father of the leader of the young gang of thugs. As a last resort, I was on the verge of involving TV and the local press when I had a message from the old lady asking me to desist, she had been warned by the father to complain no longer. My feeling of helplessness at what was blatantly unfair and unjust still makes me angry.

Apart from the wards which were solidly Labour, some of my most rock solid support came from the working class houses along the river, Tory to the core. The wealthy residents of those grand suburban residences on and around Blackheath were either wobbly in their political views, or wishy-washy Liberals. There was also one Tory gentleman who objected to me on grounds of colour, and wrote to the local press about it a number of times. When it all got too much, I wrote an open letter asking my supporters to send him to 'political Coventry' as he would appear to prefer having a Labour MP.

One mystery that remains unsolved to this day was that shortly after my adoption, it was reported to me that one distinguished constituent, John Grigg, was not exactly in favour of my candidature. He had earlier renounced his title as Lord Altrincham, and had achieved fame or notoriety by criticising the Queen in the early 1950s, earning a well-deserved smack in the face from one of her countless loyal subjects. The information came to me through one of the Association officers, who was a well-established local cobbler with His Lordship as one of his customers. I mentioned this to the then Indian Deputy High Commissioner who was also a friend of Griggs, and he telephoned me a few days later to say that it was all rubbish, and Grigg was not against me. Only recently, just before Grigg died, we happened to coincide for lunch at the Beefsteak, it was the first time that we had ever conversed, and I asked him diplomatically about it. He remembered the incident, but professed support for me. But how did the rumours originate?

John Butterfill, in the Commons at the time of writing, was the Tory candidate in Greenwich for the 1978 GLC Elections. One balmy spring evening, canvassing on his behalf, I rang the doorbell of No 1, Broad Walk, a leafy street with every promise of Tory supporters behind the well-tended garden and paths. The door opened, and a burly squat tattooed gentleman confronted me. I had just started to say that I was from the local Tory association, when he cut me short, and said, 'I know who you are; seen you on the telly, and in the local papers.'

'I hope then that you would also vote for me come the General Election.'

'Naaoow.'

'Why not?'

'I'm National Front, see.'

'Delighted to meet you; could we get together sometime over a drink to talk things over?' I enquired.

'Well, I'd have to bring my mates, and there are plenty of them.'

'Please do,' I said, knowing that there were no more than five or six in the constituency. I did follow this up, but without response.

At the next Association meeting, after the formal business had been concluded, came the time for the Parliamentary Candidate to answer questions from the floor; I knew that I was going to face a googly when the first questioner rose to his feet, an officer in H.M. Customs, a stout supporter with an impish sense of humour. 'Mr Chairman, looking at the canvassing returns for the GLC election, I would like to congratulate our Candidate on being the very first Tory ever to ring a National Front doorbell; could I ask him how he felt?'

I was thinking quite alertly that evening, and springing to my feet, said, 'Well, my first thoughts included being reminded of my first bottle of champagne, the first tiger I shot, and my first woman.' This answer was most gratifyingly received by loud applause. Driving back to Kensington that night, and in a situation not unknown to most husbands, I was chastised by my wife. 'When will you grow up?' said Stephanie, 'they don't like that sort of humour any more; you probably lost a few votes tonight.' The telephone was ringing as we entered our flat, and one of my greatest supporters, Janet Cotton was on the line, but before she could say anything, I said, 'Janet, it's past midnight, I've got to be up early to earn a living to be able to look after Greenwich, Stephie's lectured me the whole way back. I know I went a bit far with that comment about my first woman.'

'No, not at all,' said Janet, 'all of us loved that, but you should not have mentioned the tiger because I'm anti-blood sports.'

Of a number of engagements outside the constituency, I was rather flatteringly asked to participate in a debate at the Oxford Union, and although I forget the actual wording of the motion on immigration and race relations, the late Nicholas Ridley and myself were on the same side. Over a lunch prior to the set date, Nicholas said to me,' Narindar, let us agree to take a light-hearted line; after all we would be speaking to some of the greatest brains in the country, future Prime Ministers and all that; if we pursue the light touch, we'll win.' He could not have been more wrong; we were completely trounced, one of our opposing speakers going as far as to say 'I do not know why Messrs. Ridley and Saroop have been asked here; they have no knowledge of the subject.' This was Lord Avebury, formerly the Liberal MP Eric Lubbock. I don't blame him for twisting the knife. About two years earlier legislation had been enacted to oblige motor cyclists to wear helmets; the Sikhs in Southall rebelled, saying that if they were allowed to fight for the Crown in the Second World War in tanks without any other headgear except their turbans, there should also be an exception now. They got my support, as requested, and in turn I obtained young Winston Churchill's support. Sometime later, Lord Avebury accused Winston of being a racist, prompting me to write to The Times, refuting this allegation, and pointing out Winston's stance vis-a-vis the Sikhs. On the strength of my letter, Winston then filed a suit for defamation, and Avebury settled out of court. I was seated next to him at the Oxford Union dinner, introduced ourselves by pushing our place cards towards the other, and when he saw my name, he exploded, 'You are the damn man who cost me a lot of money.'

One of the other involvements, and I can't really remember exactly how it came about, was that I seemed to become the unofficial unpaid emissary between the Party and the Indian Prime Minister, Mrs Gandhi. She had then declared a National Emergency, suspending all democratic processes in India, having recently nationalised the banking and insurance industries, and reneging on the guarantees, enshrined in the Indian Constitution, given to the Indian princes in 1947. Very few people believed her when she said it had been done to save the country from chaos, whereas in reality it was to enable her to continue in office. In all this, her closest confidante was her younger son, Sanjay Gandhi, even more ambitious than his mother. The meetings in Delhi were arranged by an old friend in that city, Dipak Narang, scion of a wealthy family who had been influential in Northern India for three generations.

During one of my visits, he wanted me to meet Sanjay Gandhi, the power behind the throne, for no particular reason; and the latter in turn wanted me to meet his mother, 'because she would like it'. I was too polite to say that I had no such desire, seeing the way his grandfather Nehru had destroyed the traditional structures in India. At our first meeting when I was ushered into her presence. I cannot deny being charmed and impressed.

'Mr Saroop, I am pleased to meet you after hearing about your political involvement in England; will you take a message back from me to Mrs Thatcher?'

'If I can, Prime Minister.'

'Well, I want the U.K. authorities to stop certain Indians remitting money to India because it goes to fund Communist and other subversive publications.'

'But Prime Minister, both your father and you follow socialist policies.'

'It does not matter what I am or feel, but I've got to run the country.'

I began to warm to her, leadership should always be firm.

'Mr Saroop, how long have you lived in England?'

'About three years, Prime Minister.'

She put down the pencil she'd been playing with, looked at me in complete surprise, and said,

'But how can that be? Are you telling me that in a short three years, you are going to fight the next General Election, and as a Tory?'

'Prime Minister, your father's policies would not allow people like myself to serve the country of my birth, but the country of my adoption has allowed me to do so.'

She dismissed me amiably, and on return I carried out her wishes and spoke to Willie Whitelaw who told me to take the message back that first of all we were in Opposition, and therefore there was precious little we could do about it, and secondly as the money was being remitted legally, there was little anyone could do anyway. So back I went to Delhi, but by this time there were other reasons for these long distance flights between Heathrow and Delhi. Sanjay Gandhi was beginning to show signs of his egomania and being almost unhinged. He sent a message through an intermediary that he wanted to acquire control, for himself and his associates, of all the British companies operating in India, specifying the first few with which he wished to start – shades of an earlier Mugabe. One of these was Britannia Biscuits, subsidiary of Huntley & Palmers, where I spoke to someone I knew, Dick Palmer, director and shareholder. Quite correctly, they were having none of this. On my next visit to Delhi, I was asked to see Sanjay's chief acolyte, then reputed to be one of the most powerful men in India. I forget his name, but had to drive miles out of Delhi to his office in one of the white elephants that Sanjay was creating; a factory manufacturing the so-called 'People's Car' named Maruti. Waiting to be ushered in, I could not help reflecting that this shabby space was one of the power centres in the world at the time. I was also slightly taken aback at the sight of Sanjay's chief henchman, who wore just a dhoti, i.e. a loincloth, and bore resemblance to Mahatma Gandhi. He was quite amiable, tut tutted about Dick Palmer's reaction, saying, 'Mr Saroop, but there are others, and you must tell them all that if they don't cooperate, we shall expropriate.' I enquired about how he and I should communicate, and he said, 'But don't you know; through your Government, the British Government's Deputy High Commissioner in Delhi.' It was amusing to discover that I was not the only unofficial link. In addition to the official link through the High Commissioner in Delhi, the Foreign Office had a direct and parallel unofficial link with Sanjay Gandhi's organisation. With a degree of coincidence, I had already been asked to dine that night with the Deputy High Commissioner. He greeted me, saying, 'Narindar, I'm not sure that I should be shaking your hand knowing the hands you have been shaking this morning,' to which I was obliged to reply, 'I'm not sure I can shake yours, knowing the hands you shake all the time.'

The last time I saw Sanjay was on behalf of 'The Daily Telegraph. In one of his bouts of megalomania, he had expelled 'The Telegraph' reporter from India for writing what he thought was critical of him and the so-called Emergency Administration in India and some of its excesses including forced vasectomy. The Managing Editor or Editor-in-Chief then was Bill Deedes, now Lord Deedes, who asked for my help in getting Sanjay to see reason. The meeting with him was stormy. I advised him that Deedes had assured me that the newspaper would be even more meticulous and non-judgemental in its reports on India than it already had been. 'Tell Mr Deedes that I will provide a helicopter to take his reporter anywhere, but I must finally approve each report he files back to London.' I replied that this would be unacceptable, as everyone accepted the principle of journalistic freedom.

'What is journalistic freedom? Who is Mr Deedes? What is 'The Daily Telegraph' to defy my wishes?' was the shouting as our meeting ended, but shortly afterwards he did allow the reporter back into India with no strings attached. In many ways, he was Mrs Gandhi's Rasputin. He had married the daughter of a former Army Officer, who had been commissioned in the same batch as myself, and who was an honest, retiring gentleman. Sometime later his body was found in a field outside Delhi, and his death in mysterious circumstances was never solved. Rumours suggested that he had found out too much. Sanjay himself died subsequently in an air crash, piloting his own aeroplane.

The General Election of 1979 was set for 3rd May as Polling Day, and my guru and mentor, Lord Glendevon confirmed that Alec Home would keep his promise to come and speak for me in Greenwich. There was great excitement when my agent set about organising a hall for the Public Meeting. These have now gone out of fashion, which is rather a pity as they provided part of the fun in politics, and I have often wondered if this wàs one of the last, if not actually the last, to be held. Greenwich had not had a former or serving Prime Minister set foot in it since Mr Gladstone sat for it in the second half of the nineteenth century. A week or so before the event while I was out canvassing, the telephone rang in our Campaign Office. It was a senior Party agent from Central Office.

'We would like to help your Parliamentary Candidate, and are sending down Norman Lamont to speak for him.'

'Norman Lamont?' said my agent, 'there is no need for him. We've got Lord Home coming to address a Public Meeting next week.'

'Lord Home? What is he doing in Greenwich? He told us that he would only speak in Scottish constituencies during this campaign.'

'I don't know why; it's a private arrangement between Narindar Saroop and Lord Home.'

When he reported this to me, I advised him that his lack of tact would get him posted to another constituency equivalent to Siberia when Central Office was next considering transfers of agents.

The arrangements for the appointed evening were that my wife and I would receive the Homes and the Glendevons (Lady Glendevon was the only child of Somerset Maugham) and the rest of the platform party in the campaign office, a glass or two of champagne would be served, we would then repair to the Meeting Hall, capable of holding around 250, and word had already reached us that it was rapidly filling up to capacity. Something that should have been mentioned earlier was that a few years previously when John Glendevon had introduced me to Home, the following conversation had taken place during our third or fourth meeting.

'You will call me Alec,' said the former P.M.

'But sir, I can hardly address a former P.M. of Great Britain by his christian name.'

'I will call you Narindar; you will address me as Alec.'

This was due to be repeated that evening, but first our distinguished visitors arrived, people present were introduced, and Home and Glendevon said almost simultaneously, 'Funny how all Conservative campaign offices around the country always smell the same over all these years; must be something to do with the cleaning fluid they use.' I then briefed them with the schedule for the meeting; opening remarks from Anthony Marsh, Chairman of Greenwich Conservative Association, a five minute speech from myself, and then Lord Home to speak as long as he wished, followed by questions and answers. The former Prime Minister looked at me, and said, 'Narindar, no, this is your evening. I'm only going to speak for five minutes, the main speech is yours.'

'But, sir.'

'Call me Alec.'

'Alec, they have all come here to listen to you, they've been listening to me for the last three years, and they are bored listening to me, and I've only prepared a speech for five minutes.'

'Doesn't matter,' said Alec, 'any politician can expand a speech of five minutes into one of twenty or more.'

My heart sank, my stomach heaved, there were only five minutes to go before we adjourned to the Meeting, and then I felt a friendly hand on my shoulder. It was John Glendevon, who said, 'I heard it all; I know the old boy, once he gets up to speak he won't stop. Carry on as planned.' This is one of the biggest debts, one of many, that I owe John, combination of a wiser elder brother, a benevolent uncle and guide.

We trooped into the Hall, packed to full capacity, and the schedule of the meeting went according to plan; Chairman's opening remarks, my brief speech, and Alec's marvellous half-an-hour marathon, which was all the more gratifying because at regular intervals he would put his hand on my shoulder, sitting next to each other and say, 'and what is more, Ladies and Gentlemen, when you return my friend here to Parliament on 3rd May ...' etc. etc.

Time came for questions, and it had been agreed that he and I would answer alternately. A few questions later it was his turn, and the question was, 'What does the Platform think of the situation in Northern Ireland?'

'Over to you, my dear boy,' says Alec.

'But Alec, it's your turn,' I mumbled.

'Over to you,' commanded the former Prime Minister.

I then employed a trick that he had taught me; it gives you a few seconds to think, and puts the questioner on the defensive. 'Cup one hand to your ear, and say could you repeat the question', was the advice Alec had given me sometime earlier, and that is precisely what I did. In answer, I said, 'In my three years or more of involving myself in the issues that concern Greenwich, Northern Ireland has never been mentioned as one of concern. If you return me to the Commons on polling day, and if it is a matter of concern, I assure you that I shall brief myself in detail.' Applause, a big grin from Alec, but that was not the end of it. John Glendevon telephoned me next day to pass on his and Alec's congratulations. 'Alec feels you've got it; he was most impressed with your performance, and particularly your answer to the Northern Ireland question, but what pleased him most was that you remembered to employ the trick he taught you.'

On Polling Day, with the help of supporters and my wife, we succeeded in bringing down the Labour majority from around 18,000 to under 6,000. Having only managed about an hour's doze, I was due at the BBC studios in Shepherds Bush at 7 a.m. to a discussion programme chaired by Robin Day, along with three or four other Greater London Candidates/MPs. 'I'm pleased to tell you, Mr Saroop, that the swing to the Tories in Greenwich was 0.5% higher than the national average, and about 0.7% higher than in other Greater London constituencies.' (I'm going by memory for these figures.) 'Could you tell the audience whether you experienced any or much colour prejudice?'

My reply was, 'The incidence of colour prejudice prevalent is far less than is imagined, but more than can be identified.'

Shortly afterwards, my wife was persuaded to be the Chairman of the next annual Kensington Conservative Ball. Anyone ever involved knows the amount of hard work involved, the money to be raised, the actual organisation of the event, not least of which is the allocation and location of tables with the respective seating plans for each demanding deep thought so as not to upset anybody who might feel they had been wrongly placed; and then there was her speech as Chairman.

Obviously I gave her all the help I could, and knowing how she hates public speaking, offered to write her speech and to let her rehearse it in front of me. 'Go away, I can manage,' was the answer. I continued to be a worried man until she got up to speak. Not having been told what she was going to say, making a speech for the first time, I felt proud when she finished speaking – the content, delivery, emphasis, pauses and inflection were utterly professional. As we were filing out of the Intercontinental Hotel at the end of the evening, I heard the voice of a former MP for Chelsea, Lord De Lisle, say a few paces behind, 'I think we had the wrong candidate in Greenwich for the General Election; if it had been Stephanie, his wife, we would have won it.'

When Mrs Gandhi was assassinated in Delhi, the anti-Sikh hysteria prevailing there spilt over in various forms into English city areas where there were pockets of Sikh population, notably Southall. It was reputed that some Sikh terrorists were hiding there, and sections of the community were aiding and abetting the terrorists in India. I was telephoned from Delhi by an intermediary of Rasgotra, the Indian Foreign Secretary, later High Commissioner, in London with a message that if certain individuals in Southall, suspected of being ringleaders would come to Delhi for discussions, they would be guaranteed immunity and also safe return to the UK.

Delhi asked for my help in putting this to the individuals concerned, which I did, with mostly negative responses. However, somehow the Indian Press got hold of the story, and went to town on it, but as usual getting it mostly wrong, implying that the Tory Government was harbouring criminals.

Much as I wished to remain aloof from what was a potentially nasty situation, it proved impossible to avoid it. A delegation of relevant individuals from Southall came to see me signifying their willingness to go to India, but demanding, in addition to the guarantee from Delhi, an additional one from Her Majesty's Government , and curiously one from me as the grandson of Sir Chottu Ram, the legacy of his reputation for fairness and justice and an apostle for religious amity. While all this was going on, my wife and I went to Kashmir to stay at the world renowned Highlands Park Hotel, owned by former fellow cavalryman called Benjia Nedou whose sister was the widow of Sheikh Abdullah, the Lion of Kashmir who had been Kashmir's Prime Minister for at least two decades. During a dinner party there, one of the guests was the then Kashmir Home Minister who informed me that my grandfather had had him jailed for writing seditious articles in the second leading daily in Lahore, titled 'The Tribune'. This brief conversation was to have a curious resonance a few days later in Delhi, marring an otherwise very happy trip, full of jollity and nostalgia with old friends. This marring started when I was fastening my seat belt on the flight from Singar to Delhi, only to see the local newspaper announcing the resignation of the Chairman of the Tory Party in England – Cecil Parkinson, who was a good friend, and nor did my spirits lift when we arrived at the Taj Mahal Hotel in Delhi. My father had affectionately driven (or rather been driven, as he couldn't drive) a distance of 160 miles from Chadigah to dine with us. Over his second pre-prandial whisky, he passed me over a copy of 'The Tribune' newspaper, which had relocated to Chandigarh from Lahore after 1947. 'You better read that, and let's talk about what we should do', said my father. On the front page, in thick type were words to the effect 'Sir Chattu Ram's grandson aiding and abetting Sikh terrorists ... Narindar Saroop instrumental in influencing Home Office to provide shelter for murderers', etc. I could have ignored it, as I lived in England; my father said he was, as always, indifferent to the rantings of journalists, but we had to think about my two younger brothers, one a judge and the other a senior civil servant, whose positions could be compromised by the hysteria then prevailing. There was no choice but to rebut the allegations, with attendant possibilities of writ, legal suits etc., all nightmarish prospects. The piece had been written by a well-known and respected journalist, Kuldip Nayar, later High Commissioner in London. It therefore carried weight, making it all the more important that it should be defended. In a moment of inspiration, I telephoned a dear friend Patwant Singh, himself a well-known and successful author. Patwant phoned back to say that Mr Nayar would be happy to see me over coffee the following morning at the India International Centre. Wisely, I decided to take my wife with me. The look on Mr Nayar's face as he rose to greet me mirrored his inner surprise, 'these two can't be terrorists'. The conversation was amiable throughout, and he told us that his piece was based on information he had received from various editors of ethnic language newspapers in Southall. He could not answer why he had not contacted me before going into print with one-sided information, and accepted that I would sue these particular individuals on return to London, that he would be called to give evidence, that all this would not be helpful in his own journalistic standing and that of 'The Tribune'. A handsome apology was printed in their issue the following day, and my family and I are indebted to Patwant for his role.

11

Washington, Detroit and the 1980 Presidential Convention

A few weeks after the thumping Tory victory in 1979 General Election, the Republican Party HQ in Washington asked us to send a group of MP's, MEP's, etc to Washington as their guests. The object from their point of view was to discuss various aspects of our successful campaign, in readiness for their own Presidential campaign for their 1980 Election. Apart from all this, there was, and I hope still is, an unwritten desire for exchange of ideas and cooperation between the two parties.

I was asked to be a member of this group. Our leader was James Moorhouse MP, and possibly also an MEP at the time but certainly later. There were about a dozen of us, including Peter Beazely MP, and Bob Walter, at the time of writing in the House of Commons. During the briefing before departure we were told what was expected of us, with the meetings due with organisations like the National Security Council, the CIA, others and not the least with various spokesmen from our hosts, the Republicans. There were a number of items on the agenda, Defence, Foreign Affairs and of course party political matters. I was told that I was to be our spokesman on Defence, (partly because I was the only one who had actually worn the Sovereign's uniform), on Foreign Affairs confined to Central and SE Asia, and tactics and strategy on garnering ethnic minority votes, in which we had been successful for the first time in a General Election.

I think we were there about a week. The Republicans had made the arrangements. Each of us was billeted in a house dotted around DC, and we technically each had one Republican Senator as our host. I was pleased to be informed that my host was to be Senator Hatch, long time Senator for Utah. I was looking forward to staying with him particularly as he represented a Mormon area, is probably one himself. Having seen the film 'Brigham Young' years ago, the Mormon antipathy to monogamy has not been a cause against which I would wish to fight. Their aversion to alcohol would, of course, lead to a difference of opinion. After an uneventful flight, we were well received in Washington, except for one minor incident. Until recently, with the introduction of the awful European Community passports, all British passports had a line requiring the description of the holder's occupation. As explained elsewhere, mine stated 'Gentleman'. The US Immigration 'gentleman' examining my passport asked me to explain my occupation. I did so patiently, including Lord Chesterfield's comment to his son in his famous letters, 'A gentleman is somebody who can play the trumpet, but doesn't'. All this was to no avail, so I suggested the Immigration 'gentleman' consult a dictionary. He brusquely answered he did not have one, at which at the point of losing my temper (my best friends would not say that I was good at keeping it) I said he could ask Her Majesty's Secretary of State for Home Affairs who had issued the passport, or his own Senator Hatch who was my host in his country, or take me into custody, and risk a diplomatic incident. In a good example of the charming and gracious manners, well known all around the world, usually exhibited by US Immigration and Customs officials, he allowed me through.

There was still one more hurdle to cross, before I joined my colleagues and our reception committee outside. All cigar aficionados know that Havana cigars have been contraband in the USA since 1961, and that American customs are pretty hot on the issue. A friend in the City – I was then on the Board of Directors of a leading Lloyds broking firm – had the solution, which was applied by many in the know. The purveyors and suppliers of wines and cigars to our Boardroom had access to a skilled person in the City, who was adept at changing the bands on Havanas to a Jamaican cigar similar in size and thickness, and then putting them into a suitably sized Jamaican box, of which he had a liberal supply. His services had provided me with sufficient supplies to last me through the rigours of our Washington visit. However, the customs official going thoroughly through my luggage seized upon one of the 'Jamaican' boxes, and enquired what they were. When I answered 'Cigars', he said, 'Gee, I know that but what kind?'. I replied 'Jamaican, as the box says'. He appeared not convinced, but finally allowed me through.

When we all gathered outside, a disappointment awaited. Senator Hatch was out of town, and I along with Bob Walter had been billeted with one of his many assistants in a house in the Washington suburbs. Our host and hostess could not have been nicer and kinder, but I telephoned a friend, the Acting Indian Ambassador Ashok Gokhale, who insisted that I stay with him.

My main memory of the main meetings and discussions is that it was we who included Afghanistan on the agenda. The Americans appeared to be indifferent to it, even though this was August 1979, and all indications and intelligence suggested strongly that the Russians were up to something. But our hosts more or less shrugged off the issue on each occasion in came up; no, they didn't think the Russians were up to anything, they didn't feel there was any threat etc. We were somewhat surprised at their reactions, wondering whether this was another example of the failures of American diplomacy and intelligence.

Quite outside these officially arranged meetings, I was lucky enough privately to organise a few of my own. One of these was with Lord Bridges at the British Embassy – the former prime Minister, Sir Alec Douglas-Home had very kindly given me a letter of introduction. Another meeting was with a successful and well known American lawyer called Nimitz. I lunched with each on separate occasions, and Tom Bridges shared my puzzlement at the prevailing lack of concern about the situation in Afghanistan. Nimitz was even more certain than others that there was little or nothing to be concerned about. When a few months later the Russians marched into Afghanistan, I heard with mild amusement that Cyrus Vance, then Secretary of State had despatched his assistant, Nimitz, to Ankara to discuss the situation with the Turks. I sent a cable to Nimitz referring gently to our lunch, but never heard from him. At the time, I asked Sir Alec about how long he thought the Russians would stay. His reply was remarkably accurate – about ten years. Almost to the day in 1989, I was host at a political dinner organised at Buck's Club. Our chief guest was the then Pakistan Ambassador, Shahryar Ali Khan who also happens to be the Nawab of Bhopal. Before he started his excellent speech, he announced that he had just heard from Islamabad that the Russians were pulling out – the world at large heard this news about an hour later. In my own speech later, I said how accurate and prescient Sir Alec, also at the dinner, had been in his prediction in 1979.

During the other meetings in Washington, one particular memory remains. To the American mind, including those in command in Washington, the developing world is South America, and not the remainder of the globe that could be put in that category. To a certain extent, this is understandable because what is on one's own doorstep is of prime interest. When talking about defence, one American lady present – my notes do not reveal her name – made one of the most telling remarks of the whole week – 'You guys have to remember that your country has a centuries old martial tradition. America does not. Your mothers and sweethearts are used to bearing with fatal casualties. The American matriarch is not. When the first body bags begin to arrive home, there is instant clamour for bring our boys back'. This is deeply ingrained in the American psyche.

Next summer, in 1980, there was the Republican Presidential Convention in Detroit, and I was again one of the Tories who were asked by the Republican Party to come as special observers – a group of about nine or ten I think. This time I got my travel agent to organise a room in a hotel some miles outside Detroit – because of the Convention, hotels were packed in the city. On this occasion there were no special briefings before departure, since there were to be no particular meetings. I was impressed by the regeneration of Detroit's city centre areas, mainly due to the initiative and efforts of Henry Ford, I was told. The Convention was being held in the Joe Louis Arena, a building of several floors and on the top floor in a large space was the VIP hospitality suite, which we were kindly asked to use as our base. To go to an American Convention of this nature for the first time is an eye opener. The whole thing bore little relationship to our own more sedate party Conferences, where whether Tory, Labour, Liberal or the T.U., a number would have had apoplexy if their respective Conferences had featured drum majorettes etc. It was an enjoyable week, made all that more agreeable by being asked to various lunches and dinners emanating from some personal introductions I'd brought with me.

The last evening was full of drama, political twists, and a lucky escape. We had assembled in the VIP suite, where our host for the evening was Senator George Baker, I think then chairman of the Republican Party, and a highly likeable individual. He very kindly briefed us on what had happened that day. Ronald Reagan's presidential nomination was in little doubt, but there were still negotiations going on between the Reagan group and the advisers of Gerry Ford, the Vice Presidential candidate. The other Vice Presidential candidate was George Bush Sr., who was somewhat behind Ford in the likelihood stakes. It must have been around 9.00 pm that evening. Suddenly, over the loudspeakers came an announcement from one of the security supervisors at one of the many entrance gates, 'Hey, this is Jake, security at Gate X; there is a guy here who ain't got a pass, but wants to be let in; says he is the Prime Minister of Canada; will someone come and vouch for him, or do I handcuff the nut?'.

The conversation with Baker went on, we listened with half an ear to the announcement, which was repeated. When it was repeated a third time, Baker jumped up and said 'God, that's Pierre

Trudeau; why didn't he let us know he was coming'. Of course what had happened was that with the border of Canada so close, Trudeau must have just driven over. Apart from other considerations, it was a lapse of good manners not to have given prior notice. Baker later brought him over to us; we were introduced, but I was not impressed. Leaders should have dignity, bearing and gravitas, instead chasing after so-called charisma – which not all have – and behaving like celebrities, most of whom are entertainers anyway. Very few leaders possess these qualities these days, and no wonder society reflects this in its lack of dignity, good behaviour and style, and its diminishing respect for political leaders.

All the while, drama was unfolding behind the scenes. We learnt from Baker that the Ford camp were making near impossible demands, like requesting the Chairmanship of the National Security Council for the Vice President and similar demands. The Reagan camp had had enough, and dug their heels in. Thinking that the outcome was a near certainty for Ford, George Bush had retired to bed a few hours earlier from where he was now dragged to be informed that the Vice Presidential nomination was his.

I must have left the arena about 2 a.m. and was slightly concerned about taking a taxi out of town at that hour of the morning – having been warned before arrival about the crime situation in Detroit. However, a policeman on duty assured me it would be quite all right, and furthermore he took the number of the cab while telling him where to go. I arrived back at my hotel without incident. Having collected my room key, I felt like spending a few minutes in the hotel garden, taking in the moon and stars. It was a beautiful balmy night; to my delight, soon to be succeeded by some joyful anticipation, I was joined after a few minutes by a very pretty girl. We fell into conversation, she was intelligent, asked me about the Convention, and was obviously agog on hearing about the Bush/Ford drama. As we continued conversing, ideas, and hopes were racing through my mind, as they would through the mind of any full blooded male. I tried to steer the conversation towards my hoped for direction by asking her whether she would like to see the stock of Havana cigars in my room (she was smoking); I said, 'God, it's a bit late, isn't it, for a pretty girl like you to be down in the garden alone'. The angels must have been protecting me that night. It was rather fortunate that I hadn't gone straight into the first stage of my wooing campaign, because her answer, innocently and sweetly delivered was, 'Oh, I am waiting for my husband who is the night security guard'. As if to support it all, just a few seconds later a giant of a man came out of the shadows.

What a lucky escape! Apart from probable, if not certain, physical injury, think of the potential embarrassment, scandal, newspapers etc. the next day.

The next morning I was due to catch an early morning flight to San Francisco. I was suffering from lack of sleep and an excess of hospitality. At the Airport and waiting for the flight to be called, I decided a hamburger would revive me. While I was demolishing this, I saw someone standing over me with a camera. 'Do you mind if take your picture?' he enquired genially; I asked why. 'Well', he said, 'it's the first time I've seen anybody dressed so formally, wearing a carnation in his buttonhole, and eating a hamburger this time of the morning'. The copy of the photograph he sent me caused much amusement back in England.

I was fortunate enough to be travelling posh on the flight, and was therefore offered a choice of meals. Believe it or not, I chose a hamburger to accompany some excellent Californian wine. Receiving me at San Francisco were two friends, Wally Baird and Wally Kapcke, both members of the Bohemian Club, where they took me to lunch, taking no notice of my protests that I had already lunched on the plane. After a couple of excellent dry martinis, (my late friend Bill Channing, one time head of Time/ Life Europe used to say that he and I were born one martini short, and therefore always trying to catch up), we studied the Club luncheon menu, attended by one of the best Head waiters I have ever come across, the epitome of a black gentleman. He fussed particularly around Baird, who was then I think the Club Chairman. 'Your usual, Mr Baird?' he asked. Baird replied 'Sure, I'll have the Bohemian hamburger, I don't have to talk to a woman for three weeks.' I asked what this dish was, to be told that it had a double onion ring in it. I opted for the same, making it my third hamburger between waking up and lunch.

The reference to the three weeks without female company was because we were setting off for the Bohemian Camp, where I was to be their guest. From all I hear, there has been not a little speculation about the Bohemian Camp, and like all Clubs they wish to remain private. I hope, therefore, what I say is not breaking any confidences. The Camp lies on the bank of Russian river, some 60 miles north or so from San Francisco, in the midst of the most attractive and beautiful Redwood country. It encompasses many square miles, and within its area are several small encampments, where members have banded together in groups, convivial and compatible with each other, creating what may be described as several small Clubs within the overall umbrella of the main Bohemian Club.

These encampments are dotted around the estate, each with its own special characteristics and individuality. For example, one has the reputation of producing the best Bloody Marys, another the best cup of coffee or cocoa, while a third may provide the best music; its members being skilled amateur musicians. Each has a name, and all I can remember is the name of my own where I was a guest – called Thalia after a well known whore in the San Francisco area around the turn of the century. Our speciality was that our own bar was manned twenty four hours a day by staff brought in from San Francisco. In theory, and in practice, anyone in the whole camp, from probably a mile away could drop in, say, at 4 a.m. and be served any drink he liked, whether or not any of us in Thalia were awake to dispense hospitality. Another of our attractions was Wally Baird playing the piano – he was excellent, with a wide repertoire. I marvelled at the talents of these pillars of San Francisco society; they could probably only express them during the three weeks that the Camp functions in July, when they let their hair down.

The hub of the whole Camp centres around a charming lake alongside which is a giant Redwood tree with a large hollowed out trunk so spacious that it holds an organ. Nearby is the main dining area, in the open, of tables and benches, and a really huge board hung at some height displaying the menu of the day. Also near are telephone/fax centre, a barber's shop, and a small restaurant open 24 hours a day. There were only two meals a day – brunch available until around 2 p.m, and dinner around 7 p.m. or so. My daily routine would be to come down from a little tent a bit later than the others, who were early risers, use our encampment's communal shower facilities etc., and join the others already around our open- air bar. By then they would be well into their first Bloody Marys of the day, and we would then troop down to the dining area for brunch, a really enormous meal, which then obviated the need for any lunch.

I don't really like missing my lunch, so my brunch intake was sparse. Towards mid morning I would take long walks in the lovely surroundings which were criss-crossed all over by well maintained paths. Small mini buses service these paths, again almost 24 hours a day, ferrying members unwilling to walk some quite considerable distances. You could stop them wherever you liked to get on or off.

Wherever I might be on my walk, from around mid day the sounds of the organ in the Redwood trunk would pervade the whole camp. Many members were accomplished players, and would take it in turns to play each day. The organ recital was also a sort of trumpet call for those who so wished to gather around the lake, where there was a daily talk by one expert or the other on some interesting subject, and while I was there I had the privilege to listening on two successive days to Lee Kuan Yew and Henry Kissinger, both also guests in the Camp. Sadly, I missed Ronald Reagan's performance a few days after I left. The President Elect stayed at the Bohemian Camp shortly after the Convention in Detroit. On one of my walks one day, I bumped into Sir Michael Palliser, then Head of the Foreign Office.

I would normally lunch in the small restaurant, full of alcoholic hospitality, and enjoy, once again, an excellent hamburger. One of the walks had been quite strenuous, uphill and downhill, and the first encampment I stumbled into could not have been more hospitable. They didn't know me, I said I was from Thalia and they made me feel most welcome. The whole Bohemian ethos is a very good example of the open handed generous American hospitality, and is redolent of the spontaneous humour and wit of the America of an earlier generation which we all loved. I wish I could be as enthusiastic about what it is today.

After lunch, finishing the last puffs of my contraband Havana cigar, I would have a post prandial nap – what up to my generation in the British and Indian Armies used to be described as 'Egyptian Physical Training or Studying for the Staff College'. On regaining consciousness, I would join my fellow members at our bar, where guests from other encampments might have dropped in – in quite a few cases most interesting individuals – one of them told us of his experience and service in Vietnam. On other occasions we would drop in on other neighbouring encampments, for a drink before dinner, and I remember one particularly for two reasons. I had taken along my smoking jacket to wear in the evenings, and I heard someone say loudly enough, and deliberately so, for me to hear 'Gee, doesn't his mother dress him well?'. A good example of the sort of humour and wit Americans used to have. The other reason for remembering that visit is not something which gives me any pleasure or clubability – that whole particular encampment was dominated by a huge blown up photograph of Jackie Kennedy emerging from the water, nude and full frontal, pubic hair and all. I found it embarrassing.

Nevertheless, the Bohemian Camp is, or was, the greatest fun. We lived in the open, and looking at the moon, sky and stars in the midst of all those giant redwoods, the schoolboy in me would go into fantasies of the Apaches, Cheyenne and Sioux lurking behind them, positioned on the branches, waiting to pounce. I went to the Bohemian Camp on two occasions. My considerate and kind hosts were typical of the sort of American the world used to love – humorous, witty and mature with some knowledge of the outside world. We enjoyed our frank and free conversations; I liked their directness, they liked my cynical and understated humour. But sadly, all this was already in decline. I would have loved America but for the fads and cultish culture they have developed. My friends told me that it started mainly with the liberal educational establishment in the 1960's. They have created a lack of proportion. In 'drug awareness' classes, a heroin habit is treated the same way as a tumbler of Scotch and a quiet smoke. Smokers are considered pariahs. At the time of writing, American politicians are thinking of introducing legislation where you can't start drinking until you are 24. Maine has already legislated that it is illegal to smoke anywhere in the state where people under 21 are present, but incredibly 18-20 year olds can walk into any gun shop or pawn shop, or gun show in America and buy a handgun. If you cannot smoke until you are 21, drink until 24, the country that legislates this is postponing maturity. It is a childish and brittle society.

There was one other visit to Washington, in the mid-1980s in October. The weather was not only kinder than the earlier two visits in July and August, but the country was experiencing an Indian summer, with most agreeable temperatures and lovely sky and colours. It helped to sustain me in the fairly punishing schedule of meetings and entertainment every day. My wife and I had flown out on Concorde, and stayed very comfortably at the Ritz Carlton, a splendid hotel. Friends with local knowledge had cautioned Stephanie to avoid certain areas, even during the day when she was on her own. I returned one day, and made the normal husbandly enquiry of what she had done. When she described where she had walked – some of the streets near the White House, unsafe and frequented by whores, I was so livid that I threatened to put her on bread and water for the rest of our stay. On our last evening, there was an amusing party on board the former Presidential yacht (I have forgotten its name) on the Potomac River, on which we cruised sedately. I fell into conversation with a fellow guest who I knew was involved in fund raising for the IRA. This issue of Ireland is another one on which the Americans need a lot of educating. They genuinely seem to believe that the British are holding on to the last bit of their Empire. If only they understood the situation as it really is, perhaps they would be less likely to provide money for arms that have killed so many innocent people. I explained all this as best as I could to the gentleman, who appeared to appreciate it. On returning to London I briefed Sir Nicholas Scott MP, an old friend and then Minister of State in the Northern Ireland office, who followed up the conversation.

Towards the end of the evening, our leader Stuart Thorn came up to me and said that the he'd just heard that thanks to Sir Edward Heath, we had been allowed a half hour meeting next morning in New York with Henry Kissinger. We couldn't be a large group, he was restricting it to three in number. A helicopter had been arranged, we would leave around 6 a.m., and return to Washington in the evening. My wife and I were booked to return to London on the Concorde flight that same evening, and when I weighed up the tight transfer timings the next day, and my fatigue, I just did not feel strong enough to do it; I have regretted it ever since.

There was one particular attraction for us to be on board the Presidential yacht. During the War, one of the cabins had been used by Sir Winston Churchill during his Washington visit. This had been offered to my wife and I for our stay, but we decided to wallow in the luxury of the Ritz Carlton Hotel.

Those days, UK passport holders required a visa to visit the United States. I had one which allowed me an unlimited number of visits, and was valid indefinitely. When my passport ran out of paper due to my frequent travels, I applied for a new one, and my secretary sent it along to the American Embassy with one of our company chauffeurs - an excellent man called Jimmy James who had served with the Middlesex Yeomanry during the War, and the tank that he had been driving had been the first ashore in the British sectors of the Normandy beaches. He returned shortly afterwards, looking embarrassed and said, 'I don't know why Sir, but the Yanks would like you to go in personally with your application'. The prospect of joining the large queues outside the Embassy in Grosvenor Square did not appeal. I picked up the phone to Bill Channing (former European head of Time/Life), tracked him down to the bar at White's Club, and explained my predicament. 'Somebody will telephone you very shortly, Narindar', said Bill. Within fifteen minutes my phone rang and it was somebody, whose name I have forgotten, from the American Embassy. 'Mr Saroop, I am the Head of Station in the UK' (CIA or Immigration, I never found out), 'and I am very sorry about what has happened. We pride ourselves in having well educated staff who issue visas. Something went wrong in your case. I've just had a call from Washington instructing me to issue your visa. On your application form you had filled in the question about reasons for visiting the USA as political and business. Our staff read that as political business, and wondered whether you were going there to be involved in subversive activities. If you would send the chauffeur back to me ...'.

This was American efficiency and friendship at its best. A call to a friend, who calls Washington, who call the Embassy, who call me – all in under a quarter of an hour.

12
'Clubs, Friends and a Few Enemies'

All my life, I have wanted to add to my rather limited vocabulary. I love learning new words, not a new interpretation of an old word, where, in modern parlance, the original meaning has been stood on its head, at times to mean the complete opposite, the best or worst example of which is the old innocent word, gay. During one of the meetings of the Council of the Institute of Directors when I was serving on it, a new word came my way. It was networking, and was used many times that morning. During the lunch adjournment, I buttonholed one of the Institute's executives to enquire, and the answer was, 'Well sir, it means getting to know people, the sort of thing people like you do in your Clubs.' I was obliged to tell him that Clubs were meant for like-minded individuals, with either a shared background and/or a shared experience, that you didn't join them to get to know the members; you knew a number already and they knew you, as otherwise they probably wouldn't have you. Some years later, I was in for another surprise because you couldn't open a newspaper without some trite item about 'Celebrities go out clubbing'. With my slow peasant mind, it took some time for the intelligence to filter in that what they were referring to was the new generation of discotheques or night clubs, where I would have been turned away at the door.

I was brought up with Clubs being a part of the life of everybody one knew, starting with my father. One of the many British bequests to India, after the Indian Army and the railways etc, is Clubs. I recall my father's generation going to their Clubs almost every evening, perhaps just for a quick drink with chums, or to play a hand of bridge, possibly for lunch one or two days a week, and certainly on ladies evenings when members were allowed to bring lady guests. As a boy, being driven past these impressive entrances, I so looked forward to the day when I may be allowed to enter. A gentleman and his Club were taken for granted, which reminds me of another two new words that have entered the English vocabulary, i.e. house husband. It was amusing to discover what they meant. My mother would have had a fit, and my wife would still think that there is something wrong if I didn't look into one of my Clubs every single day, when I am in London. I would have thought that it aids marital bliss to have the husband out of the way, and not in the house all the time.

My first Club was in the military station of Ambala, while still in my teens as a young army officer. This was the Sirhind Club, named after a nearby river, the ancient channel of which had completely dried up. There was a cocktail dance every Wednesday, a dinner dance on Saturdays when you were expected to wear a dinner jacket, and various other gala evenings like Christmas and New Year's Eve, which were full dress affairs. It was such fun to go up to a pretty girl and say, 'May I have the pleasure of the next dance, the Regiment sails at dawn?' when the sea was over a thousand miles distant. Almost every town and city had, and still has, a Club, but I've never come across anywhere with the same number of Clubs as Calcutta. There was the Bengal Club, meant entirely for Chairmen and Directors of British Companies, there was the Bengal United Services Club, meant for senior Civil Service and military officers above Field Rank, the Calcutta Club meant for the top echelons of Calcutta society, British and Indian, Royal Calcutta Golf Club, Tollgunge Club (golf, racing and social), Calcutta Swimming Club, Calcutta Rowing Club, Calcutta Squash Club, Calcutta Football Club, Calcutta Cricket Club, Saturday Club (social), 300 Club (based on the old 400 in London), Calcutta Bowling Club, the Armenian Club, the Punjab Club, the Marwari Club, the Sikhs Club, the South Indian Club, the Parsi Club, and last but not least, the Calcutta Scottish Country Dancing Club – I know that I have left out quite a few like the Calcutta Light Horse Club. There was no legislation in those days to prosecute the South Indian Club if they refused to take a Sikh mad enough to want to join, still is not, and I hope will never be.

The country's capital, New Delhi, compared poorly with all this. There were only two major Clubs, the Imperial Delhi Gymkhana Club (local Whites) and the Chelmsford Club (the local Boodles). When I was proposed for membership of the former, Col. Bromhead the Secretary enquired of my father whether I could afford to pay its bills on my young officer's salary.

The position about the colour bar in some Clubs during the Raj has never been fully and accurately understood. No doubt it was hurtful, no doubt it contributed to hastening its end, but there were some logical reasons behind it. Besieged by protocol and to show the stiff upper lip most of the time, the British needed a place to relax with their own kind. With Indian women still in purdah, their men would have gone to the Clubs on their own, feeling the anxiety that Englishwomen would be enticed away. It was the superior airs practised by the civil servants, middle class, and their rather suburban mem-sahibs that added salt to the wound. Curiously enough, this was not the case in most of the military stations, where the Clubs were dominated by the Army, and British and Indian officers serving in the station mixed easily and freely, with even the Indian wives joining in. The leading London Clubs probably never operated a colour bar; the Maharaja of Burdwan was elected to the Carlton Club in 1904, Prince Duleep Singh having preceded him by three or four decades, and there were Indian members of the Cavalry Club from the 1920s onwards. The old Guards Club had a Chinese member, an officer of the Grenadiers, in 1940.

Now, fair damsels are at the gates, battering on these remains of civilised male bastions. As somebody said, 'Why do women want to go where they are not wanted?' Weaker forts have fallen, surrendering to the combined assaulting forces of nagging ladies, a politically correct climate, and a number of members within turning Quisling by weakening the defences to allow in the conquering hordes. I am very pleased to say that two of my Clubs have not surrendered, never will, as they fully appreciate that the ethos, jollity and spontaneity would never be the same. Clubs manage to be homes from homes, with longer-serving staff as friends, without the delicious presence of ladies. At an all-male table for lunch or dinner, there is loud, jolly, frank, possibly boisterous and schoolboyish conversation, at times also informative and erudite, but introduce Marilyn Monroe into the company, there is a marked change in the atmosphere. Where else in the world would you hear the likes of an exchange between two people except in a Gentleman's Club that I was once privileged to hear.

'Hello Robert, I hear you've been to New York.'
'Yes.'
'Did you see my ex-wife there?'
'Yes.'
'Did you take her out to dinner?'
'Yes.'
'Did you take her to bed?'
'Yes.'
'My dear chap, come and have a drink.'
I'm not sure that in celebrities' clubs, the corresponding conversation may not run as follows.
'Oi, you, you been to New York?'
'Yeah, man.'
'You shagged my ex-wife then, din ya?'
'Honestly mate, I never touched her.'
'You bleedin liar, take that and that and that.' Enter the bouncers.

The dictionary defines the word 'normal' as 'conforming to the standard, regular, usual, typical, free from mental or physical disorder', but I wonder how many people have known or met a really normal individual. Each of us has some quirk or the other, even without any major aberrations or abnormalities of character. More by accident or chance than design, most of my deep and abiding friendships have been with people older than myself, and all considered somewhat eccentric. Therefore I have few remaining, but I have also, more unconsciously than consciously, followed Dr Samuel Johnson's advice, 'Sir, the state of friendship must be kept in constant repair.' There were many friendships at school and in the Army; it is curious that in retrospect they were not so deep. Two of these were the late Maharaja of Patiala and the Raja of Nalagarh, who were relations by marriage before they became friends.

H.H. Patiala had two passions, botany and cooking. He asked me once to meet him in Paris, but instead of the fun and jollity to which I was looking forward, we seemed to spend most of the time in visiting one nursery after another. Staying with him in Motibagh (Garden of Pearls) Palace, he would suddenly decide over aperitifs, 'Let us have a moonlight picnic at Pinjore', which was a lovely garden from Moghul times, with terraced lawns, flowerbeds and waterfalls, but about forty miles away. Servants would be despatched to one of his properties and everything would be beautifully arranged and laid out, tables and chairs, with places laid, and an open air kitchen in one corner, the chefs awaiting His Highness's arrival, because he insisted on putting the finishing touches to each of the several dishes. We would arrive in a convoy of a number of cars, having driven for part of the way without lights in the brightly moonlit countryside, continue to get inebriated since His Highness's finishing touches meant that dinner would not be served until after midnight. There were enough bedrooms at Pinjore for those so wishing to sleep it off there, but my wife and I always drove back to the Palace, sometimes arriving at dawn. It was fortunate that she was a good driver, well known on the hill roads for coming round bends in a jeep at rash speeds, with one leg hanging elegantly out of the vehicle. We both had a passion for speed.

Potatoes have been an equal passion, family and servants despairing at my lack of interest in vegetables. Tobacco is another favourite, and although I gave up cigarettes on leaving school, I discovered the delight of cigars some years later. It has therefore been a particular privilege to have enjoyed the deep friendship of someone whose forbear by marriage, Sir Walter Raleigh, introduced both the potato and the weed into England. Sir Walter had secretly married one of Queen Elizabeth's ladies-in-waiting, Miss Throckmorton, and both were subsequently banished from Court. Sir Robert Throckmorton (it is incorrectly spelt as Throg-morton Street in the City), 11th Bt. stayed a very dear friend for over forty years until his death in 1989. Known as the Sleepy Baronet or as the Dormouse, he had an alert and razor sharp mind which added to his spontaneous wit. The family seat was Coughton Court near Stratford-on-Avon. The family acres on which William Shakespeare had been apprehended stealing an apple were sadly depleted by the time he inherited as a schoolboy, but he still owned the whole of Exmoor that does not belong to the Forestry Commission, and the enchanting North Devon village of Molland, where it was a joy to stay. His passport had stated his occupation as 'Retired' since 1930, when after Sandhurst and a spell in the Grenadier Guards, he decided enough was enough. The only other time he tried to work was when Guardian Insurance appointed him as an Agent. During the short tenure of this appointment he was dancing one night with the heiress Barbara Hutton, married at the time to Count von Reventlow, her third or fourth husband, and he suggested that her fabulous jewellery might be insured. 'Darling Robert, would you take care of that for me? It's all too tiresome,' said Barbara Hutton. Robert had never woken so early as he did the next morning, sped to the Guardian's offices, had some details worked out, and appeared at the Ritz for lunch, as arranged. Count von Reventlow was the first to appear, and said, 'Sir Robert, I understand you are going to insure my wife's jewellery. If there is any commission, I shall take it.' It put Robert off from working for the rest of his life, and he decided to call it a day. At a dinner party in London one evening, one guest was saying rather pompously, 'If one can't make love to a brother officer's wife, who can one make love to?' 'The brother officer', said Sir Robert Throckmorton.

We were fellow guests in Jaipur one year, sitting in one of the drawing rooms at Rambagh Palace after dinner, when Robert was casually flicking his cigar ash, some of it still aglow, onto the beautiful Persian carpet. 'Do stamp that out, Robert, its ruining the carpet,' said our hostess, the world-famous H.H. The Maharani of Jaipur, described as one of the most beautiful women in the world in the 1950s and 1960s. 'But what about my shoes?' was the riposte. Robert was timelessly, quintessentially English, and I could not help but weep unashamedly at his funeral.

Dining one night with Gibby, the present Earl of Minto, and two other friends in a West End establishment, we were making rather a lot of noise in celebrating the birth of Minto's heir. A few tables away were the Duke and Duchess of Windsor, when the third person at their table came over to us and enquired which one of us was Lord Minto, because His Royal Highness would like a word with him. Poor Gibby, expecting to be chastised, staggered towards H.R.H., who kept him standing.

'Minto, are you by any chance one of my godsons?'
'Yes, sir.'
'Good, good, celebrating the arrival of an heir, what?'
'Yes, sir.'
'Good, good; tell me, Minto, did I ever give you a present, what?'
'No, sir.'
'Wallis, make a note, a present for my godson, another for his heir.'

Minto, father and son, waited in vain for any present to appear.

As much as Robert Throckmorton was my introducer to England, I was blessed with having the late Sir Iain Moncreiffe of that Ilk in getting to know Scotland, and the late Lord Dunsany similarly for Ireland. Iain was a well-known genealogist, with a phenomenal memory. 'White Mischief' the book about the murder in

Kenya of his late father-in-law, the Earl of Erroll, had just been published, and we were staying with him in Perthshire when reporters started besieging him. Asked if he was the biggest snob in the British Isles, he replied that there was nothing wrong on anybody's part to know and learn more about their family ancestry. The next question 'What do you feel about the Queen, Sir Iain?' brought the reply, 'If she were plain Miss Elizabeth Windsor, I would marry her.' He dropped in unexpectedly one evening in London when we were entertaining someone passing through, H.H. The Maharaja of Suket. I had barely finished the introductions when Iain said, 'Your Highness, your grandfather unsuccessfully pestered Queen Victoria to increase his gun salute from 11 to 13 guns.' Suket's jaws dropped, he was unaware of this fact. Iain's book 'History of the Highland Clans' is a landmark in erudition. As someone once said of him:

'And so for miles around the wonder grew
That one small head could harbour all he knew.'

Herald, genealogist, advocate, scholar, courtier and clubman, Iain was surely one of the most colourful, funny and engagingly eccentric characters that the monochrome twentieth century has produced, and he took some pride in being descended from 'Countess Dracula', the infamous Elizabeth Batory who murdered 600 young girls in order that their blood might magically preserve her beauty. His descent from her, as Iain delicately put it, was 'via a legitimacy hiccup and a Croatian serf.' So much far flung intelligence, wonderfully recondite knowledge, erudition, humour and sound commonsense sadly died with him at his death in 1985 at the early age of 65.

The first time I went to Ireland was to stay at Dunsany Castle in Co Meath, not many miles from Phoenix Park. Kindly collecting me at the airport Lord Dunsany informed me that he'd like to show me around Dublin, followed by lunch at the Kildare Street Club before finally heading for the Castle. In the city's National Portrait

Gallery, or equivalent, he pointed to a picture of the Irish patriot Michael Collins being lowered into his grave. 'Mark that belt around his middle,' said my host about the Sam Browne belt officers wear with their Service Dress, 'it started its career at Sandhurst around my father's middle in the 1890s, went through the Boer and First World Wars. When the Irish troubles started in the 20s, my father always wore uniform, and returning one day to the Castle, he heard the sound of gunfire. Ordering the chauffeur to drive to the sound of the guns, the car was ambushed by the I.R.A., and overturned into a ditch; no serious casualties, but one of the I.R.A. personnel pointing his gun at my father lying in the ditch, said, "I'm sorry, my Lord, I hope you are not hurt; but could I have your belt please?" It stayed with him just a few hours, being then appropriated by a sergeant, then by a junior officer, then successive senior officers until a few days later it adorned the figure of Michael Collins wearing a civilian suit with a military Sam Browne. When The Troubles were over, my father wrote to Collins asking for his belt back, to which Collins replied that he had grown rather fond of the belt, but would return it on the condition that should he die before His Lordship he would like to be buried in it. As history records, Collins was assassinated a bit later, my father kept his word and there you see the belt around Collins' body.'

On a balmy summer morning, while staying at Dunsany Castle, his wife, the Dowager mother and myself were enjoying a glass of Pimm's on the lawn in front of the main door. Around 11.45 a.m. there were footsteps on the gravel, and my host came into view wearing striped trousers, black jacket and a Homburg hat and passed us without saying a word. While still within earshot, Lady Dunsany shouted out

'Randal, where are you going?'

'The City.'

'But we've got Narindar staying.'

'I know, I asked him to stay.'

'We've got guests to lunch in just half an hour.'

'I know,' and he was gone, and we saw his Mercedes tourer start down the drive. At the appointed time for the guests to arrive, I was in the library when Randal came in dressed in tweeds and ready to receive his guests. Nothing was said about his movements; when he said 'the City' did he mean London or Dublin? In any case this was impossible in the time involved. One could speculate that he might have been visiting a mistress on his estate, and that it was customary to dress in formal clothes on these occasions.

Lt. Col. the Hon. Randal Plunkett, as he was before he inherited as the 19th Lord Dunsany had served in Guides Cavalry in the Indian Army before and during the War, and prior to its outbreak had been sent on a one week's Demolition Course for Officers. In customary fashion, there was a fancy dress dance in the local Club on the Saturday, and Randal came dressed as a corsair, patch over one eye (he usually wore a monocle anyway), bandanna handkerchief wound over his head and carrying a pickaxe. Having consumed two whiskies and soda, he brought the pickaxe down on the bar and proceeded to smash it into pieces. When it was all over, he looked around the room and said, 'And after all that, the damn fools failed me in demolition.' He had a good War, as they used to say, serving with his Regiment in the Desert, where for one particular act of gallantry and courage he should have either been awarded the Victoria Cross, or court-martialled for disobeying orders. Sadly, he was undeservedly cheated out of the first, and fortunately avoided the second. Details may not be of much interest to non-miliary readers. Stories of his eccentricities and foibles were legion amongst those who were fond of him. We both used the same hairdresser at the Cavalry Club, and I used to be regaled from time to time about His Lordship's latest 'bon mot'. In his last few years, hair grew out of his ears in profusion.

Barber: 'May I clip these, My Lord?'

'Certainly not; leave them alone, they keep out the Irish mosquitoes.'

For eleven of the happiest years of my life, I was on the Board of a leading Lloyds' broker, H. Clarkson & Co, which is now called Aon Insurance. I owed this to an introduction from Michael Craig-Cooper to Charles Muller , who happened to be a political colleague, former Mayor of the Royal Borough iof Kensington + Chelsea, and Chairman of the Committee which planned and commissioned our impressive new Town Hall just off Kensington High Street.The Chairman was a splendid chap to work for; Jeremy Peyton-Jones, an old Etonian, member of both Whites and Boodles, and who had never used public transport in his life. He was particularly understanding and supportive over the time I had to spend on my constituency and other political duties. One day I happened to mention during a Boardroom lunch that I had unwittingly crashed a red traffic light near the Oval the previous evening returning from Greenwich, been stopped by a Police Car but had fortunately got away with it. He glanced at me across the table, saying, 'The Company will provide you with a chauffeur driven car during the Election. I won't have you involved in anything that could be embarrassing.' As far as I can remember Sir John Loveridge and I were the only two Tories to fight the 1979 Election with chauffeur driven cars, although I always got dropped off and picked up outside the constituency to avoid any Press comment. But there was a debit side to his munificence. He ordered that the small refrigerator in my office containing all essential liquid refreshments which all Directors had in their offices, would be temporarily withdrawn, but that I could use his own, only a couple of doors away. One morning, as I was pouring out my vodka and tonic, he was finishing off his dictation. 'Now Jean, a final letter to the secretary of X Club enclosing my cheque for entrance fee and subs etc. etc.' Jean shut her book, left the room, and I couldn't resist pulling his leg by saying, 'But Jerry, the X Club is mainly for actors,' at which he said, 'If you hadn't already poured out the vodka, I would have forbidden it. Get out of my room'. A few days later the office chauffeur collected me after lunch at the House of Commons, saying we had to pick up the Chairman as well, but not from one of his usual luncheon haunts. It was not a Club to which he would have liked to belong, and when seated together I couldn't again resist saying,

'Jerry, I'm worried about you; first you join X Club and now you lunch here.'

'Major (his usual form of address when he pretended severity) I'll have you know that X Club was founded to bring actors together with gentlemen.'

'Chairman (responding to his Major) every schoolboy knows that, but in which category do you put yourself.'

'Jimmy (to the chauffeur) stop the car, let the Major alight and walk back to the City.'

The most honourable and upright person I have known, and had the privilege of his friendship was Lord Glendevon. Born as Lord John Hope, he was the younger twin son of a former Viceroy of India, the Marquess of Linlithgow, and as he used to say, 'What a difference being five minutes late into the world makes to the rest of your life.' In the 1930s, the only two young men that debutantes' mothers allowed to take their daughters out without chaperones were the two Hope boys, John and his elder twin, Charles. They were considered that honourable. In the words of another friend, 'John was a life enhancer,' a good mimic with a marvellous sense of humour. One of the many legends in the Scots Guards was the story about a training exercise on Salisbury Plain in late 1939, where John was one of a number of fellow officers under instruction.

'Gentlemen, in front of you is an expanse of dead ground hiding the enemy. On his right and left are machine gun posts, and it is possible that they might have tank support soon. In planning your next moves, what is the first thing you'll do, Lord John?'

'Write home and ask mother,' was the reply from Hope.

Inasmuch as a number of my friends were somewhat raffish, John was the steadying hand in my life, to whom I always turned for advice and guidance, and his wise counsel and support was never withheld. First returned to the House of Commons in the 1945 Election which was disastrous for the Tories, and entering the Chamber in his first few days, he had to pass Winston Churchill, who motioned John to sit beside him. 'I would like you to be my Parliamentary Private Secretary,' growled the great man.

'It's a great honour, Leader, but may I think it over?'

'Think it over? Such an opportunity; well, let the Chief Whip know.'

When telling me the story, John said that there was no way he was going to personally serve Churchill, who had made his father's life hell as Viceroy by scheming with the Indian Princes to complicate and delay Linlithgow's attempts to bring about Federation, the next step towards Indian freedom. I asked him about how and what he said when declining Churchill's offer. 'By writing him a very polite note saying how flattered I was to be offered this great honour in my first week in the Commons, but I must learn to stand on my own two feet first.' Churchill never forgave him, and it was Macmillan who later created him a hereditary peer in one of the last of such creations. His brother, Charles, by then the Marquess of Linlithgow sent him a congratulatory telegram, 'Welcome to the noble house,' to which John replied, 'Thank you, but at least I have earned it.'

Having never harmed anyone in my life, except the odd unkind word on occasions, yes, because I suffer from a short fuse and a low threshold of boredom, it was with some surprise that I learnt that I had two enemies, one socially and the other politically. When I was advised of the existence of the first and that he was strongly against my candidature of a particular Club where I had the support of over 25 members, John Glendevon asked me of any possible reason. 'I've only met him once, when we were introduced in the bar of the old St James's Club in Piccadilly. He seemed very knowledgeable about India, and particularly various Viceroys, so in all innocence I asked him on which Viceroy's staff had he served. He replied rather crossly that he had never been on any Viceroy's staff, but usually only stayed with them.' And that was all, but he felt that I had insulted him.

The second gentleman then held a senior position in the Tory Party, and was subsequently to hold one of the highest political offices in the land. Alec Home asked me to take him head on, and enquire what he had against me. I telephoned, and was asked to come and have a drink. He was affability itself, strongly denied that he was an enemy; but two comments in our amiable conversation gave him away. Firstly, he said that I should learn that in politics one's enemies are in one's own party, the Opposition benches were only full of political opponents. Secondly, he said that in common with others he regarded me as a 'Pukka Sahib', whereas he was not sure that he was looked at by all in the same light. 'Pukka' in the Urdu word for genuine, true, solid and so on, 'not ersatz.' He recited the following Cavalry jingle:

> The Regiment at Poon-AH
> Would definitely soon-AH
> Play single handed polo
> A sort of solo polo
> Than play a single chukk-AH
> With a chap who isn't pukk-AH

It also got back to me that in some conversation in the Whip's Office, he said, 'Look at this fellow, Saroop; he gets asked to stay in houses around the country where I have to pay to get in.' While professing to be one of my greatest supporters, he had taught me a valuable lesson, i.e. that one's enemies are usually in one's own camp.

The curious thing was that both gentlemen were essentially non-English. In the case of the first, his forbears had left Baghdad only two generations earlier, whereas the second's were from Mittel Europe. Prejudice lurks in strange places, quite often with people who complain about experiencing it themselves. Whatever may or may not be said behind one's back, I have never encountered any racial prejudice in England, only friendliness and kindliness.

13

The Destruction
of Two Cultures

While still a child, I was in our car being driven through Amritsar, the Sikh holy city where the Golden Temple is sited. We went past a statue of Queen Victoria, and pointing it out, my grandma said to me, 'It was from her reign onwards that women in India could safely walk or travel alone'.

In 1998, my wife and I were staying with friends some miles outside Delhi. There was a village a comfortable walk away. My host told me that only a week before our arrival, there had been a tremendous commotion one evening, the most identifiable strand of all the noise being female shrieks in distress. He sent his gate-keeper – a former soldier – to investigate. On his return the tough veteran was in tears. He said, 'Some local politicians are having a public meeting tomorrow in the neighbourhood. Their followers are rounding up women from nearby villages for the politicians' pleasure. How can this happen just a few miles from the capital of India?'

Not so long ago, my wife could blithely walk through Kensington Gardens and Hyde Park on her way to and from her office in New Bond Street. It made no difference if it were dark. Quite sensibly, she now desists.

How did it come to pass that the capital of one of the largest Empires in history, and the capital of its erstwhile Jewel in the Crown should deteriorate to this state? These personal experiences are comparatively small straws in the wind, or a gale, that has been flowing through both these intertwined cultures, since the 1950s in India, and the 1960s in England. In India, it is not difficult to see how and when it started. Since the 1920s the British Raj was the easy and obvious target for the fighters for Indian freedom, but behind all that there was also their separate agenda for social reform. The two went hand in hand, and it would be difficult to argue with the intrinsic worthiness or value of both objects. The social reformers of that generation were not only some well-intentioned middle-class intellectuals – or 'useful idiots' as Karl Marx described that ilk – but a number of Rulers of the erstwhile princely States. H.H. Sir Sayaji Rao of Baroda and H.H. The Maharaja of Mysore are notable examples. In their territories some social reforms, like women's education, were ahead of such affairs in adjacent territories of British India. And Reform was also taking place at what might be described at a sensible pace in most of British India. Then there was the deluge of 1947 with the bloody Partition of the country. With one of their objects gained, irrespective of the cost in human lives, and the division of the country which could have been avoided, the successors of the earlier gentler well-intentioned spokesmen, turned with zeal and haste to social reform. The good intentions remained, and admittedly a great deal of the reform was overdue, but it was all carried out in great haste as if there were no tomorrow. The people around Nehru were not all idealists, but had their own objectives. I am sorry to say that some of the remaining Indian members of the Indian Civil Service – described as 'heaven born', the creme de la creme of all the Civil Service cadres in the whole Empire – were excessive in their zeal to bring about these reforms, and aided and guided their new political masters with enthusiasm. The Indian Civil Service with British and Indian members was by and large a great blessing to the country, and a credit to its members. Their hierarchal and organisational structure, with the District Officer on the lowest rung, leading up to the possibility of a Governorship of eight out of the 11 Provinces. (Bengal, Bombay and Madras were described as Presidencies for historical reasons to do with the President of the Court of Directors of the East India Company where the Governor was usually an aristocrat appointed directly by London, and not somebody who had risen to the top of the Civil Service Order in the other eight provinces. Lord Brabourne, who died while in office in Calcutta and was reputed to be a likely successor to Lord Willingdon as Viceroy is an example.) Digressing slightly, after the Labour Government won the 1945 landslide election, it sent out a former Railwayman as Governor of Bengal to succeed Sir Reginald Casey. Frederick Burrows, the new Governor knighted before he set out for India arrived as Sir Frederick Burrows. Nobody quite knew why the new government in London had done this. He had no experience or knowledge of India, perhaps they were cocking a snook at the second city of the Empire where Grandees like Wellesley, Minto and Curzon had left their mark, but he did have a sense of humour. I met him once, at the annual Calcutta Dinner in the Connaught Rooms near the Aldwych. He was most affable and likeable.

The Indian Civil Service was the iron framework which kept India well-administered and well-governed. But a number of the senior members in the Government of India secretariat in 1947, and by then almost entirely Indian, had fairly large sized chips on their shoulders. In their service they had wielded authority and power, almost entirely honourably and to general benefit, but a number had come up against the influences and popularity of the local minor or major aristocracy. They had resented this, and this resentment had been transferred in their minds to the Princes.

It was with some glee that they threw themselves enthusiastically into aiding Nehru in his plans to destroy the Princely and established order. Only their brilliant minds, honed by years of experience in administrative and legal matters could have brought about so quickly the end of the Princely states, picked off one by one using the carrot and stick principle. The Labour Government ditched the sovereign treaties which each Princely State had with the Crown in 1947; by 1951 the Indian Civil Service, under command of their new political masters had eliminated all of these from the map of India. The new political orders wanted to combine democracy with a controlled economy on the Soviet model. Again, the civil servants, realising how this would increase the powers of the bureaucracy, drafted one Five Year Plan after another, each of which increased the stranglehold of the State on almost all industrial and economic output. A new factory could not be started without applying for an Industrial Licence, applications for expansion had to endure their passage through a number of Government departments, Central and State, and be vetted within the framework of what had been decreed by the Planning Commission. Years were spent on trying to replace English as the lingua franca. This ended up with the compromise that all the business of the Central Government would be carried on in English, whereas the business of the different State Governments would be conducted in the language of each; when corresponding with Delhi they would attach an English translation to all their communications, and vice versa. In the last decade there have been attempts to liberalise the economy, and although at senior political and bureaucratic levels this desire appears to be genuine, the story is not quite the same at more junior levels.

Nehru's passion for socialism was unalloyed. I think he took the initiative in asking his friends in our Labour Party here for the services of Economic Advisers for his Planning Commission. Two gentlemen with reassuringly English-sounding names called Balogh and Kaldor were duly seconded to Delhi, where the local wags promptly christened them as Bulganin and Khrushchev. They performed their duties splendidly, and came up trumps with the idea that in addition to Income Tax, there should be a Wealth Tax and an Expenditure Tax; in other words, your capital was going to be progressively reduced, and on whatever income you had left after paying income tax, a further tax had to be paid if your expenditure exceeded a certain amount. Fortunately, even the Socialists saw how unworkable this new system was, and it was scrapped after a few years. Not unusually, all these controls encouraged corruption, which although present at junior bureaucratic levels, but almost entirely absent at political levels until 1947, is now rampant. It is no longer a matter of shame to be suspected or convicted (unlikely) of corruption because almost everyone is involved. To get a decision or ruling on any matter from the appropriate senior bureaucratic and political levels, the particular file has to move up the line. Unless those at the bottom are bribed, it will lie unnoticed or simply disappear. Bribery is again required to get favourable comments at various different levels, because the chap at the top will not rule, whatever the merits, against earlier comments for fear of all being accused of corruption. A rather interesting example of the lack of any standards was that of a Minister in Nehru's Cabinet who had not filed his Income Tax returns for many years. When tackled in Parliament, he said that pressure of duties and work had made him forget. No action was taken, with the matter quietly dropped.

It is a moot point whether the layers of bureaucracy were foisted on India by the British – as claimed by the Indians – or whether their experience in India planted the fondness for it so evident in Britain today. The truth is that the British in India built upon the systems inherited from the Mogul Empire, and got saturated enough to bring it back with them. It is not quite within the remit of this book to indulge in a serious analysis of the factors that brought about the destruction of their respective traditional cultures in India and England. I say England not only because this was the usual way to refer to the British Isles when I was growing up and maturing, but because Sir Richard Body's analytical and discursive book, 'England for the English' is a valuable source of reference on what has happened to England and why – but what I would like to point out briefly is what I have seen and experienced myself. Whatever else, I feel that encroaching socialism has been a common factor in both countries. It may be hasty or even wrong to make a judgement on one individual's experiences, but nevertheless these are indicative of the way things were going, living through the changes – in the main to the detriment of society – that started making themselves manifest in the 1960s. Perhaps Beatlemania is the appropriate word to describe the abandonment of standards, judgement, and wisdom gained through not only a unique social structure that worked, but also the worldwide experience through the Empire. Beatlemania has produced what its supporters say is a dynamic society. When I question what this means, the most coherent answer I get is, 'Everyone is on the move, you can do what you like, there are no rules, who wants rules, man? Everyone does his own thing.' This so-called dynamic society has rejected values, in the home, in schools, in business and in almost every walk of life. This continuing Beatlemania, with its offshoot descendants, has in the past 40 years also changed England almost out of recognition – the exceptions, fortunately, being the Armed Forces, to some extent our Police Forces, and the Judiciary. Starting with the House of Commons, through the Civil Service, the City and Industry, standards of behaviour, personal dignity and reputation, the will and corresponding fortitude to set an example for others to follow, have been eroded to an almost non-existent remnant lump. As a minor example the gas inspector was somewhat a figure of fun, but because one of my directorships was involved with the Gas Industry, I came across a number of them. They were invariably bowler-hatted and carried an umbrella – amusingly ridiculed by Bernard Cribbins in his song 'Hole in the Ground'. But nevertheless they had an appearance of authority representing Authority. Things got done. When contemporary gangs are digging holes in the street where I live, and I wish to know what is happening by asking them, 'Who is in charge here?', the answer is likely to be 'Hey man, let us do our own thing'.

Harold Macmillan said that the country changed when people stopped going to Church on Sundays. I would add a rider and say that also when people stopped asking who was in charge, because nobody now appears to be so, or if actually in existence would not wish to admit it. Is it a sign of change in our national character that while more and more people disclaim responsibility, more and more are progressively moving towards the American compensation claim culture? 'The child is the father of man'. Does this partly explain progressive surrendering of the English way of life to the American ethos? ·

In one of the many penetrating points made by Richard Body in his 'England for the English', he suggests that with the end of Empire, the English character is reverting to its original Anglo-Saxon prototype, and builds up a good case for this. However the independent and sturdy Anglo-Saxons did not have to deal with too many trouble-makers or enemies in their midst; where there were any, they must have got short shrift. And of trouble-makers and enemies within, we have had many in the last 40 years. The early Bolshies proliferated in the unions, probably still do, but they were not difficult to identify. Much more dangerous, and also still with us in possibly increasing numbers are the breed that have been infiltrating the teaching profession, journalism, local government, voluntary organisations and other activities. Having had personal experience of this, recounted earlier in this book, I would claim familiarity with their tactics. They have two main objects in which they have been regrettably and noticeably successful. The first one is that in situations which they cannot control, the intention is to create as much confusion and disruption as possible, probe for the soft and vulnerable points, pierce them and then try to obtain control. The second is where they are in control already; then to fill these organisations with like-minded people. The Race Relations bodies are good or bad examples. In the mid 1970s it was suggested to Mark Bonham-Carter that I might assist him in his capacity as Chairman of the newly-founded Race Relations Board. He was willing, but was thwarted by the cadres then entrenched in the organisation. They did not want someone who was not 'one of them', and it is certain that similar tactics have been followed in many other quangos. The question could well be asked about how this was allowed to happen by those in authority. If Labour were in office, it was of little concern to them. When the Tories were in office 1970-74, and for eighteen years between 1979 and 1997, they neglected this, failed to address the issue, and Mrs Thatcher paid scant attention to one quango after another – she had undertaken to do away with them, but actually allowed more into existence – being packed by appointments of Liberal and Labour nominees, but rarely Tories.

In fact, authority and firm leadership have been on the run since Beatlemania and with the growth of satire. Left to itself, satire can be very funny indeed, but there is a new element of viciousness in its portrayals, resulting in diminution of authority. 'Who is in charge here?' itself became a question ridiculed out of court, and the savaging of Alec Douglas-Home by the media, particularly David Frost in his television interview could all be described as a pattern. We have loved satire for some centuries, enjoyed it, but it lacked the vicious streak it now has. Attempts to destroy the traditional leadership – itself now a term of ridicule, if not abuse – have succeeded, the longed for meritocracy has taken over, and the ambitions of many politicians across the political spectrum has been achieved. But has this really made society or our lives any better? Whether it is public services, education, local or national government, or indeed any walk of life, the criteria of efficiency, standards and value for money have all seen a marked deterioration. Financial scandals in the City, big business and over the pond in America with cases like the collapse of Enron were almost unheard of before meritocracy took over. The best run businesses are still family controlled and family run. When the meritocracy take over, they feel that they own the show, and not the shareholders. If a family business is badly run it folds, whereas with the PLCs of this world, glaring errors are covered up, those responsible leave with a golden handshake, their replacements are brought in at even higher salary packages, and others who were culpable but not exposed can always find a priest's hole in the organisation to continue their management of mediocrity – meritocracy often equals mediocrity.

But there is an even darker side to meritocracy in the effect it is having on individuals and their mental state. In a meritocratic age, because it is felt that the successful truly merit their success, it follows that the failures are exclusively responsible for their failures. The question of why, if one is in any way good, clever, or able but is still poor becomes more marked and painful to answer for the unsuccessful. In this new age, the poor have moved from being described as 'unfortunate' to being described as failures, targets of contempt in the eyes of the self-made individuals who feel disinclined to shed crocodile tears for those whose company they have only recently escaped, and who should recognise that they have an inferior status. To the injury of poverty, a meritocratic system adds the insult of shame.

Although not entirely or primarily responsible, Mrs Thatcher cannot entirely escape blame or responsibility for, at the very least, not discouraging the coming about of this state of affairs. She was a forthright patriot, 'a demon, but my God we need her', as a senior Tory politician put it, but in the longer term she contributed to the current eclipse of the Tory Party since 1997, by removing one by one the traditional Tories in the Parliamentary Party, and making it a party of meritocrats, resulting in people like Archer, Hamilton and others who contributed to the accusations levelled at it as 'a party of sleaze'. Blair has, of course, taken the concept of the meritocratic society even further with his botched attempts to reform the House of Lords. The voting public should ask what is the point in meddling with the best second chamber in the democratic world, one which has historically proved itself, costs comparatively far less than the Commons or anything that would replace it, full of well-intentioned individuals with experiences encompassing every facet of British life from salmon fishing in Scotland to being a bus driver, a policeman, a diplomat or a soldier.

People will always respect those whose ancestors did something for their country and were rewarded as a result. Ah! but because they inherited they do not fit into a meritocratic framework. Even the much vaunted meritocrats have a quotient deficient in their successful make up. Having derided the principle of heredity in their climb up the rungs, they suddenly realise that they have to employ expensive accountants and solicitors to try and ensure that the wealth they earned by their meritocracy deserves to be passed down by the principle of heredity. There was an old saying 'The worst tyrant is a small or mean man in a position of authority'. We have all experienced them, in offices, banks, local government, police, airports or behind the telephone call, and when at last we get a human voice, he or she refuses to divulge his or her name. These sort of people have always been there, but a meritocratic age has entrenched their mediocrity and authority. It was a blessing to grow up in a pre-meritocratic age where those in command kept mediocrity in check.

Another facet of meritocracy is the cult of youth, which has resulted in young people in the prime of their lives worrying about being put on the shelf after they pass 30 years or so of age, all this adding to status anxiety. The age of the individual should not be a major factor in being considered for a job. The only criterion should be 'who is the best person available for this particular job?' irrespective of age, sex or colour. Mr Greenspan, who has been deciding U.S. fiscal policy for years is, I think, around 78 years of age, which may not necessarily always bring wisdom, but certainly brings experience, so that when there is a difficulty or a crisis, there is someone around to say what happened the last time. The right combination or mix should be the vigour of youth and the experience of age.

Beatlemania and associated trends led to a lowering of standards not seen before. A doctor was pointing out the dangers and social nuisances of binge drinking amongst the young, with some of them vomiting in the streets. A meritocratic young lady interrupted to say, 'What does it matter? Somebody will clean it up. Let them do their own thing.' No wonder that the unusual sighting of a policeman on the beat no longer inspires confidence in the law-abiding, or fear in the law breakers.

Society is becoming ungovernable, politicians perhaps deservedly have lost respect, the media is all powerful, but has no authority. This blurring of edges in all directions could be a possible scenario for the emergence of an authoritarian state. I think Shake-speare wrote somewhere, 'Take but degree (rank) away, untune that string, and hark! what discord follows', or words to that effect.

Is it not curious that wealthy Asians now send their children to schools in India, whereas up to the 1970s or so it was the other way round? Socialism has not yet killed good education in India, and I am heartened by a letter recently received from a friend there. 'We had elections in six States; in one region of Rajastan, Maharani Raja, a real Princess won, and the so-called Queen Sonia Gandhi's (Nehru's great daughter-in-law) nominee lost.' It is ironic that whereas socialism appears to be beginning to lose its hold in India, in England since 1997 its earlier trotting or cantering pace has accelerated into a gallop. The ethos of political correctness in Britain is totally alien to the natural ethos of this country. Freedom of speech was one of a number of characteristics which made us a unique nation.

Most people do not realise to what degree it has been stifled by stealth. What is the point of inventing terms like 'vertically disadvantaged' to describe short people. Blair's babes and boys will say it shows a caring society. A truly caring society does not drive free speech underground. If I were short, and heard somebody referring to me as 'vertically disadvantaged', I would shout out 'I prefer to be called Lofty, mate.' Do not the exponents of political correctness realise that in suppressing free speech they are unwittingly or otherwise treading a path where the 'Caring Society' for which they care so much gets more and more vulnerable to authoritarianism, as political correctness progresses?

The wicked fairy at my birth decreed that I was not to be a man of my time. I have little regret about this, and although this has been a misfortune in many ways, the blessing has been to have grown up, lived and matured before Beatlemania and Political Correctness. I would have liked to live in Elizabethan, Restoration, Regency, or Edwardian times, and in Indian terms, the reigns of the Emperors Akbar and his son Jehangir.

On the odd occasion of a bout of insomnia, I lull myself to sleep imagining a conversation with God when I die. I have been blessed with a strong faith as long as I can remember, and also have a firm belief in rebirth and reincarnation; not the nonsense about coming back as a bird or an animal, but coming back exactly at the same level of consciousness and inner development that is there at one's last breath. When we wake up each morning, we are the sum total of everything we were up to the point of sleep the previous night. Today will add, amend or subtract on that for tomorrow and so on. It is rather difficult therefore to accept that all life's experiences will be extinguished at death. There will never be any proof, of course, just belief and faith. Naturally, I feel I deserve to go to Heaven. Knocking on His Gates, and having dodged St Peter,

God:'What are you doing here?'

Self: 'I wish to remain with you, my Lord, and not return to Earth.'

God: 'That remains to be seen; let Me have a look at your Balance Sheet; you were a very good son.'

Self: 'Thank you, my Lord.'

God: 'You were a good father and brother, and also good to your friends.'

Self: 'Thank you my Lord.'

God: 'Were you a good husband?'

Silence.

God: 'Answer.'

Self: 'My Lord, both my wives have said I was loveable, and I hope they quite understood the joy my company provided for others of their gender.'

God: 'Well, you have not yet earned the right to remain with Me; why do you not wish to return to Earth?'

Self: 'It is governed and ruled by mediocrity as never before. Political correctness has made it a rather boring place. The lowest common denominator controls the way of life, even in the manner in which You are worshipped.'

God: 'It is not for you to criticise my Creation. Very well, you have not yet developed enough to remain here, but I shall send you to another planet.'

Self: 'Thank you, my Lord."

Reverting to Richard Body's 'England for the English', I am optimistic that in the next few generations the Asian immigrants would have melted almost entirely into being English, much as happened with earlier waves through earlier centuries. My message to them, public and private, has always been the same; 'It is in your interest, and in the interests of your descendants to support and maintain an England which is strong, internally and externally. It is your duty to support England's institutions, the Monarchy, Parliament, the Judiciary, the Armed Forces and the forces of Law and Order, because these are the glue that keep England strong, internally and externally. If you cannot support the other institution, the Church, remember that England exercises the greatest toleration for other churches to practice.'

Who does not love the land of his birth? I love India. But I also love England passionately. I would fight for it to the last round of ammunition and to the last drop of my blood. I mean for Her Majesty's England, but not for Blair's Britain.

Finally: the happiest man in the world is one who employs a butler to arrange appointments for family members to see him.

Index